SAIS
PAPERS IN INTERNATIONAL AFF

The Making of Foreign Policy in China

WESTVIEW PRESS / BOULDER AND LONDON
WITH THE FOREIGN POLICY INSTITUTE
SCHOOL OF ADVANCED INTERNATIONAL STUDIES
THE JOHNS HOPKINS UNIVERSITY

NUMBER 9

SAIS
PAPERS IN INTERNATIONAL AFFAIRS

The Making of Foreign Policy in China

Structure and Process

A. Doak Barnett

WESTVIEW PRESS / BOULDER AND LONDON
WITH THE FOREIGN POLICY INSTITUTE
SCHOOL OF ADVANCED INTERNATIONAL STUDIES
THE JOHNS HOPKINS UNIVERSITY

A Westview Press / Foreign Policy Institute Edition

Copyright © 1985 by The Johns Hopkins Foreign Policy Institute, School of Advanced International Studies (SAIS)

Published in 1985 in the United States of America by Westview Press, Inc., Frederick A. Praeger, Publisher, 5500 Central Avenue, Boulder, Colorado 80301

Library of Congress Cataloging in Publication Data
Barnett, A. Doak.
    The making of foreign policy in China.
    (SAIS papers in international affairs)
    Bibliography: p.
    Includes index.
    1. China—Foreign relations—1976-   . I. Title.
JX1570.B37   1985   327.51   85-3319
ISBN 0-8133-0232-3
ISBN 0-8133-0233-1 (pbk.)

Composition for this book was provided by the William Byrd Press, Richmond, Virginia, for The Johns Hopkins Foreign Policy Institute, SAIS
Printed and bound in the United States of America

10   9   8   7   6   5   4   3   2   1

The Johns Hopkins Foreign Policy Institute (FPI) was founded in 1980 and serves as the research center for the School of Advanced International Studies (SAIS) in Washington, D.C. The FPI is a meeting place for SAIS faculty members and students, as well as for government analysts, policymakers, diplomats, journalists, business leaders, and other specialists in international affairs. In addition to conducting research on various policy-related international issues, the FPI sponsors conferences, seminars, and roundtables.

The FPI's research activities are often carried on in conjunction with SAIS's regional and functional programs dealing with American foreign policy, Latin America and the Caribbean Basin, Africa, the Middle East, the Soviet Union, U.S.-Japan relations, Canada, security studies, international energy, the Far East, Europe, and international economics.

FPI publications include the *SAIS Review*, a biannual journal of foreign affairs, which is edited by SAIS students; the SAIS Papers in International Affairs, a monograph series which is copublished with Westview Press in Boulder, Colorado; and, the *FPI Policy Study Briefs*, a series of analyses on foreign policy issues as they develop. For additional information regarding FPI publications, write to: FPI Publications Program, School of Advanced International Studies, The Johns Hopkins University, 1740 Massachusetts Avenue, N.W. Washington, D.C. 20036.

ABOUT THE BOOK AND AUTHOR

Until recently, Westerners have not adequately understood the structure of the PRC's policymaking process in the post-Mao period. Dr. Barnett's pathbreaking study provides comprehensive information on how China's foreign policy decisions are made. The author draws not only on his past research but also on intensive interviews conducted during 1984 with a wide range of Chinese officials (including Premier Zhao Ziyang), academics, and journalists to describe a major shift in top-level decision making from the Politburo and Standing Committee to the Party Secretariat and State Council. He analyzes the foreign-policy roles of various specialized party and government organizations, as well as the roles of key government ministries and the military establishment, and discusses not only the institutions and individuals involved in the policy process but also the sources of information and analyses on which their decisions are based, including major press organizations, research institutions, and universities. Taking advantage of the new openness of both leaders and working-level specialists in the PRC, Dr. Barnett has written the most detailed and up-to-date study available.

One of the most distinguished China experts of our time, A. Doak Barnett was professor of government at Columbia University and a senior fellow of the Brookings Institution. He is now professor of Chinese Studies at the School of Advanced International Studies at The Johns Hopkins University.

CONTENTS

ABBREVIATIONS

CASS   Chinese Academy of Social Sciences
CPIFA   Chinese People's Institute of Foreign Affairs
MOFERT   Ministry of Foreign Economic Relations and Trade
NCNA   New China News Agency
NPC   National People's Congress
PLA   People's Liberation Army
YCL   Young Communist League

PREFACE

THIS VOLUME PRESENTS in systematic form information I have gathered during the past two years on the structure and process of foreign policy making in China. Although I have studied Chinese foreign policy continuously for thirty-five years and have written a number of books and articles on the subject, until recently I, like most of my colleagues, have known very little about how and where foreign policy is made in Peking. Starting in 1982, however, I found that more and more Chinese, both officials and scholars, were willing to discuss certain aspects of foreign policy making, so I decided to gather data on the subject, primarily through interviews and conversations with knowledgeable Chinese. In 1984 I proposed to the Chinese Academy of Social Sciences that I visit Peking specifically to interview people in the Communist Party and the government, academic and research institutions, and press organizations on this subject. The academy invited me to make the visit, and its staff was extremely helpful in arranging a wide range of meetings in Peking during July and August 1984.

This study is based primarily on what I learned during the past two years, especially from the interviews.

The study analyzes the structure and process of foreign policy making, focusing on the institutions and individuals involved. In addition, it throws some new light on the policy-making process in a broad sense—that is, on where, in the Party and governmental structure, foreign policy issues are dealt with, what kinds of relationships exist among the institutions involved, who some of the key policymakers are, and where they obtain information and analyses on the basis of which to consider foreign policy issues. The study helps clarify who is involved and where foreign policy is made. Why and how specific foreign policy decisions are made is much more difficult to determine. However, because of the increasing openness of the Chinese about discussing policy-making in Peking, it may be easier in the period ahead to learn more about specific decisions as well as about the structure and general process that led to them.

In discussing the roles and relationships of institutions of special importance in the policy-making process, I identify some of the key individuals involved and discuss briefly their backgrounds and careers. The data I obtained on top Party and government leaders are from published biographical sources (cited in my notes); much of the information on other individuals discussed in the study came from the interviews in Peking. The profile of the leadership involved in policy-making should be regarded as a snapshot of the situation in mid-1984. At this writing, some personnel changes have already taken place (a number of these are indicated in my footnotes), and in the immediate period ahead there will be many more. However, these changes are likely to be in line with major trends discussed in the study—that is, toward a more technocratic top leadership increasingly composed of individuals with specialized knowledge and administrative experience in particular fields and toward greater professionalism at lower levels.

I would like to express my deep appreciation to the Chinese Academy of Social Sciences for the assistance given to me on my visit to Peking in the summer of 1984, and to the numerous Chinese officials, scholars, and journalists both in China and abroad who helped me understand the foreign policy–making process in Peking. I also wish to thank several American specialists on China who read and commented on early drafts of the study, all of whom helped me avoid some errors and improve the manuscript, though none of course bears any responsibility for the final product. They include: Carol Lee Hamrin, Harry Harding, Donald W. Klein, Kenneth G. Lieberthal, Lyman Miller, Douglas P. Murray, Michel Oksenberg, Douglas Paal, and Robert Suettinger. I am also grateful to Kristen E. Carpenter, managing editor of the Foreign Policy Institute Publications Program, and her successor, Nancy McCoy, who edited the manuscript; and to my staff assistant, Barbara S. Bowersox, who assisted me at every stage in the preparation of the manuscript and compiled the index.

For the information of readers unfamiliar with different systems for the romanization of Chinese names and terms, the pinyin system has been used (except for "Peking," the traditional Western spelling of China's capital city). I provide the romanized titles of a few Chinese foreign affairs institutions and journals that may be unfamiliar to Western readers and are not readily available in other Western sources.

1.
INTRODUCTION

IN THE POST-MAO PERIOD China has been undergoing a remarkable process of reform and development. One result has been a significant change in the way policy is made. The field of foreign affairs provides an example of changes that have been taking place more broadly in the structure of Chinese policy-making. Although it is impossible to make generalizations about the entire policy process, because the situation varies from field to field, nevertheless, recent trends affecting foreign affairs do throw light on how these changes are influencing the ways in which Chinese policies are adopted and implemented in a variety of fields.

A great deal has been written by Westerners about Chinese foreign policy over the past three decades, but little of it has dealt with its structure and process. The reason is simple. Until recently, the Chinese have been reluctant to reveal details about policy-making. This has now begun to change, however, and many Chinese, both leaders and working-level specialists, show a new openness—in itself an important indicator of political

1

trends—about discussing the policy process in Peking. Consequently, although one may not yet state with absolute confidence exactly where and how specific, major Chinese foreign policy decisions are made (it hardly needs noting that often this is also true in more open political systems), the new information that recently has come to light helps illuminate some important aspects of the structure involved.

In attempting to understand policy-making in any country, it is essential to ask certain basic questions. At the top of the political system, what individuals, groups, and institutions play key roles in decision making, and what are their respective roles and relationships? Where does their information and counsel come from? At operational levels, what mechanisms exist to coordinate the major institutions involved in the conduct of foreign policy? How influential are experts and specialists, and through what channels are their opinions voiced? Until recently, the outside world had little information with which to answer these questions, or even to make informed guesses. Foreign policy making in China appeared to take place in a "black box." One could see what policies emerged from the box, but not what went on inside it. Now it is possible to provide partial answers to such questions.

Trends Affecting the Policy-making Process

The information now available indicates that several important trends have been under way in the post-Mao period. Even though ultimate decision-making power on foreign as well as domestic policies is still highly concentrated—with one individual, Deng Xiaoping, playing a pivotal role—among the political elite, the basis for making major policy decisions has been considerably broadened.

The policy-making process is more systematic, regularized, and rationalized than it has been for many years. Most major policy issues receive careful consideration by a variety of institutions before decisions are made. At the top, there has been a very important shift in the locus of decision making and in the roles played by leading Party and government institutions in the policy process. According to authoritative Chinese sources, the Politburo and its Standing Committee are no longer in charge of most day-to-day policy-making, as Western observers have generally assumed. Today the Party Secretariat and the "inner cabinet" of the State Council, apparently working in close cooperation, are the key centers for policy-making on most issues (although they consult closely with Politburo members—especially those on its Standing Committee—on an individual basis).

As China's foreign relations have steadily expanded—in the economic and cultural as well as political realms—the problems facing Chinese leaders have become increasingly complex, requiring the increased involvement of numerous bureaucracies in China's foreign relations. In response, Chinese leaders are trying to improve the existing mechanisms for coordinating policy and to develop expertise to deal with new problems.

There is a new emphasis on professionalism in foreign affairs, a trend that has involved changes in personnel policies, organizational structures, and training. Gradually, steps are being taken to improve the quality of official information and analyses on foreign affairs. A major effort is also being made to expand and improve research on policy-related issues, both in Party and government institutions and in China's scholarly community.

The direct input of China's working-level experts and specialists into the policy process clearly is increasing, and there is a growing "foreign affairs community" in Peking, in which both official and academic specialists on particular foreign policy issues are linked through numerous personal and institutional contacts.

Some of these developments are relatively new, and the structure of the policy-making process is still evolving. Numerous problems still exist—many of them comparable in some respects to those confronting other major countries. Coordination of the diplomatic-political, economic, and military institutions involved in foreign affairs still appears to be relatively weak, especially at lower levels. The coordinating mechanisms are less well-developed or institutionalized in China than in many other countries, including the United States (where, it should be noted, they also have weaknesses). Moreover, even though the information and analyses reaching Chinese leaders appear to be improving because of more extensive contacts abroad and stepped-up efforts to strengthen policy-related research, China's decision makers continue to rely to a considerable extent on what, in the United States, would be considered "raw" data, in contrast to "evaluated" research and analysis. Despite Peking's concerted effort to place younger, more professional specialists in responsible positions in the foreign affairs apparatus (and an increasing number of these have had professional experience and training not only in China but also abroad), well-qualified people are still in short supply. The disruption of the educational and research fields and the temporary decline in Chinese diplomatic representation abroad during the Cultural Revolution compounded this problem; China's effort to improve its training and research capabilities has really just begun.

Nevertheless, as China has moved toward more active participation in the international community and has adopted increasingly pragmatic approaches to foreign affairs, the overall trend has been toward the creation of a better-organized and more effective foreign relations apparatus.

2.
TOP-LEVEL POLICY-MAKING INSTITUTIONS AND INDIVIDUALS

IN MOST NATIONS, ULTIMATE POWER to make decisions on major foreign policy issues is fairly concentrated; usually only a few leaders manage foreign policy; frequently, one person makes the final decisions. Even in the United States, despite the dispersion of power and complexity of the foreign policy process, key foreign policy decisions are made by the president and a small group of his closest policy advisors.

In China, decision making on major foreign policy issues has been even more highly concentrated. Few details are available on how foreign policy was formulated in the Maoist era, but some Chinese who were involved in or close to the process at that time now say that Mao was totally dominant and made almost all of the "big decisions." Zhou Enlai, premier from 1949 until his death in 1976 and foreign minister from 1949 to 1958, was in charge of the conduct of foreign affairs. Unquestionably, he had a significant say in foreign policy formulation. However, some Chinese who were close to Zhou at that time now stress that Mao's dominant role, especially in making broad strategic decisions on foreign policy, greatly overshadowed that of Zhou.

Nevertheless, until recently most Western scholars assumed that in most periods a great deal of decision making at the top in China was collective rather than individual, and that the Politburo and its Standing Committee made most of the key decisions on foreign as well as domestic issues. It was widely assumed, also, that in most periods the Politburo met regularly and frequently, and that the Standing Committee probably convened even more often. (In the Soviet Union the Politburo meets every Thursday, and many observers have assumed that the Chinese Politburo operates in a similar fashion.)

This is the way the system ideally is supposed to have operated in China, as in other Communist countries. The Party's primacy over the government has been clear, and the policy-making supremacy of the Politburo and Standing Committee (at least in periods between the infrequent Party plenums and congresses) has been specified in Party documents.

To what extent this was true in different periods is uncertain, however. The system may have worked fairly well in this fashion during most of the 1950s, but it is not clear to what extent reality matched the ideal thereafter. From the early 1960s on, the roles of the Politburo and the Standing Committee appeared to change; they appeared to lose power in some respects, first because Mao and other leaders relied heavily on Central Committee work conferences to deliberate on important issues, and then because Mao asserted his personal domination over policy and all institutionalized processes were disrupted. During the Cultural Revolution the entire political system ceased its normal functioning; Mao and special bodies such as the Cultural Revolution Group assumed control over many functions formerly exercised by the Politburo and the Standing Committee. After the Cultural Revolution, the latter were reconstituted, and in the early 1970s they again became important policy-making bodies. Most of the previous Party leaders had been purged, however, so that these institutions were very different from what they had been in earlier years. Moreover, in the 1970s changes in the Politburo were much more frequent and numerous than in the pre–Cultural Revolution years.

When steps to reinstitutionalize and stabilize the system were taken in the immediate post-Mao period, the Politburo and Standing Committee once more appeared to be the institutions where important policy decisions were made. However, this apparently was true for only a short period of time, and it is unquestionably much less true today.

Zhao Ziyang on the Structure of Policy-making

In a July 1984 interview that focused on how and where Chinese foreign policy is made, Premier Zhao Ziyang revealed that, even though individual Politburo members continue to play key policy-making roles, a very significant institutional change has taken place in the pattern of top-level policy-making. Day-to-day decision making on major policy issues has shifted from the Politburo and its Standing Committee to the Party Secretariat, headed by General-Secretary Hu Yaobang, and the State Council, headed by Zhao himself. Zhao stressed that these two bodies cooperate closely and that both look ultimately to Deng Xiaoping, who makes the final decisions on many issues. According to Zhao, while the active members of the Politburo and Standing

Committee continue to influence policy, they have been superseded in most day-to-day decision making by the Secretariat and State Council. (One can only speculate about when this shift took place; almost certainly it was quite recent, probably some time after the Twelfth Party Congress in September 1982.)[1]

Premier Zhao's statement on the roles and relationships of China's top decision-making bodies is perhaps the frankest and most explicit ever made by a Chinese leader. When asked if the Politburo's Standing Committee holds regular meetings, he said: "No. The daily functioning of our government machine [structure] rests with the Secretariat and the State Council."[2] Even the Politburo itself, he revealed, "does not have regular meetings." It "only holds meetings," he said, "when there are some major issues to be discussed." Politburo meetings now are held only infrequently, according to well-informed Chinese, and apparently they generally are convened upon the initiative of the Secretariat, although members of the Standing Committee can request that a meeting be held. "If the Secretaries of the Secretariat think there is a need to hold a Politburo meeting," Zhao said, "they can propose that one be held." He went on to say that "if the members of the Standing Committee of the Politburo think that it is necessary to hold a Politburo meeting, they can do that in their own right," but Zhao added that "in recent years there has not been such a case."

Zhao stressed that this represents a generational shift in the pattern of decision making when he observed that the Politburo holds meetings only irregularly because "most of the members of the Politburo are aged," so they "can only concern themselves with major issues."

Zhao noted that Deng Xiaoping has explained on many occasions that the Chinese leadership is now divided into a "first line" and a "second line." He then declared: "Comrade Hu Yaobang and I are on the 'first line'. Deng Xiaoping, Chen Yun, Ye Jianying, Li Xiannian [the four other members, besides Hu and Zhao, of the Standing Committee], and other comrades are on the 'second line' ", adding that "there are only a few issues that are determined by them."

However, Zhao made it very clear that Deng continues to play a crucial personal role in Chinese policy-making. "As all people know," Zhao said, "major issues are determined with the participation of Comrade Deng Xiaoping . . . not because of his position . . . [but because of] his rich political experience, wisdom, and prestige."[3] According to Zhao, the Secretariat and State Council also consult constantly with the other active members of the Standing Committee on an individual basis, even though the Standing Committee does not meet as a group to make collective decisions. "Whenever there is a major issue," he said, "we go to Chen Yun, Li Xiannian, and Deng Xiaoping for advice" (although he indicated that Ye Jianying is no longer actively involved in policy-making: "Marshal Ye," he said, "is old and not in good health").

Zhao's views on the relationship between the State Council and Secretariat in the process of making decisions on foreign policy were revealed when he stated that "the Party is only concerned with major issues, not concrete ones." He emphasized, however, that ultimate policy-making authority rests with the Party, not the government. "On the whole, the major issues are handled by the Party, and the State Council is in charge of routine work." He stated, though, that many of the items on the Secretariat's agenda are proposed by the State Council. "The major issues discussed at the Secretariat meetings are usually put forward by the State Council,"

Zhao said, adding that "whenever the State Council thinks that certain issues are of great importance, it will raise them with the Secretariat to be discussed."

Zhao also took pains to emphasize that the Secretariat and the State Council work closely together. After pointing out that "among the members of the Standing Committee of the Politburo, I am the premier, and Hu Yaobang is the general-secretary," Zhao stated: "I keep in close touch with Comrade Hu Yaobang, so our machine works smoothly." He noted that "I myself also participate in meetings of the Secretariat."

One can, of course, wonder if Zhao's description of China's top-level institutions in charge of foreign policy making accurately represents the reality, or simply reveals what he would like the reality to be. However, interviews with many Chinese officials and specialists involved in China's foreign affairs community indicate that a shift in the locus of day-to-day decision making has, in fact, occurred and that this shift has important implications for the policy-making process—and for the substance of Chinese foreign policy as well.[4] The general picture of the structure of top-level foreign policy making today follows.

Deng Xiaoping's Role

Deng Xiaoping remains the ultimate source of authority for making policy decisions in China—on foreign as well as domestic issues—even though he has not occupied the highest formal positions in the Party or government. Most really major decisions are made by him, and all must be acceptable to him. Deng has deliberately, in a step-by-step fashion, delegated large areas of responsibility to other leaders—especially to Hu and Zhao, men he has placed in power because they share his basic policy outlook. Nevertheless, he himself continues to be very actively involved in making foreign policy decisions.

It is not entirely clear, however, what kinds of issues are considered important enough to require his direct, personal involvement. Broad issues that are "strategic," including those relating to China's new "independent foreign policy" and "open door" policy, clearly fall into this category, as do problems that relate to China's most important bilateral foreign relationships—especially those concerning Chinese policy toward the Soviet Union and the United States. If there are significant implications for China's relations with the superpowers, Deng will involve himself directly in the details of some issues that might on the surface seem to be of secondary importance. Nevertheless, according to knowledgeable diplomatic and Chinese sources, as Deng has aged he has deliberately shifted responsibilities to Hu and Zhao and has supported their efforts to consolidate their own institutional bases.

On some foreign policy issues, Deng has been not only the "court of final appeal" but the initiator of new moves. For example, the concept of "one country, two systems," which now underlies Peking's approach to Hong Kong and Taiwan, is said to have been Deng's own idea. (The Chinese maintain that issues relating to Hong Kong and Taiwan are domestic rather than foreign policy issues, but they obviously have major foreign policy implications; the Chinese now maintain, in fact, that the "one country, two systems" concept could even-tually have important implications for China's views on how to deal not only with Hong Kong and Taiwan but with the problems of other divided nations as well.)[5] On some major issues, however, leaders other than Deng are said to have played significant roles in the process of defining China's current policies. For example, while Deng has favored a more outward-looking foreign economic policy since at least the mid-1970s, Chinese accounts of the evolution of Peking's current "open door" policy indicate that, as this policy has evolved, Hu and Zhao as well as Deng have played important roles in pushing, step-by-step, to broaden China's opening to the outside world.[6] Similarly, in the redefinition of Peking's basic international posture that resulted in the adoption of an "independent foreign policy" in 1982, not only Deng but others including Hu Yaobang and Hu Qiaomu (helped by working-level foreign affairs specialists from the State Council and academic community) are said to have played roles in formulating official statements on the new posture.[7]

On all foreign policy positions that lack a solid consensual basis, Deng unquestionably plays an extremely important personal role in making compromises and building the broad coalitions needed to support them—and to neutralize actual or potential opposition. He is in a unique position to do this. Since late 1978 (some would say 1980 or 1981) he has enjoyed primacy as China's top leader and has demonstrated great political skill in promoting his policies, compromising when necessary, and at times retrenching, but working steadily to expand the basis of support necessary to move forward.[8]

Consensus and Differences at the Top

Well-informed Chinese in Peking's foreign affairs community maintain that in recent years there has been less controversy, generally speaking, over foreign policies than over domestic policies, but there clearly has been some opposition to certain policies—both at the top and at lower levels of the regime—including policies toward the Soviet Union and United States as well as China's opening to the West. (Most Chinese officials and academics are unwilling to discuss with Westerners the possible policy differences among their top leaders in specific terms, and they criticize the "speculations" about them by Westerners, but the existence of differences among leaders is apparent in some of their public statements.)

Some members of the Politburo Standing Committee almost certainly have held views that have differed from Deng's on important foreign policy issues. Li Xiannian, for example, issued statements in early 1982 that seemed implicitly to question Deng's tilt toward the United States, and he appeared to argue for a less confrontational approach to the Soviet Union.[9] The articulation of China's "independent foreign policy" not long afterward seemed, however, either to have satisfied those with such objections or at least to have neutralized views of this sort. (Chinese who support the new posture argue that one important reason for its adoption was the fact that any appearance of alignment with either superpower inevitably evokes opposition in China and that, therefore, adoption of a middle position has helped to build a broader base of support for China's overall foreign policy. They maintain that, as a result, the consensus on foreign policy is stronger now than it was two years ago, and that it should continue to broaden if present policies are continued.)

There also is good reason to believe that both Ye Jianying and Chen Yun have had doubts about China's "open door" policy—or at least about the extent to which it should be extended—because of fears about its possible political and social as well as economic consequences. However, the skeptical view has not pre-vailed, as is clear from Peking's recent moves to open China's door still further to the West.

Personalized or Institutionalized Decision Making?

One can argue that because Deng's individual role continues to be paramount in policy-making in China, the situation is still comparable in some respects to what it was during the Maoist era, because ultimate decision-making authority is still personalized rather than insti-tutionalized. However, the differences are probably more important than the similarities. Deng's methods of operating contrast greatly with Mao's. His basic ap-proach is to build coalitions in support of his policies rather than simply to impose them by fiat on others. As a result, he has been more successful than Mao was in his later years in constructing coalitions that provide solid foundations for his policies. Moreover, Deng now is attempting to use his personal power to institutionalize policy-making gradually (however much this may seem to contradict his exercise of personal power) and to move from individual to collective decision making. He also is attempting to differentiate the functions of the Party and the government more than in the past, to ensure a greater role for government in policy-making.

The recent shift in the locus of much decision making—from the Standing Committee and full Polit-buro to the Secretariat and State Council—has contrib-uted to these objectives. Not only has it helped to neutralize opposition to Deng's current policies, it also has contributed to the process of institutionalizing policy-making, to the transition from personal to collective decision making, and to the strengthening of the role of the government in the policy process. Informed Chinese stress that the most important result of the shift is that it has laid the groundwork for an orderly succession and an eventual transfer of power (at the time of Deng's death, if not before) to Hu and the Secretariat and Zhao and the State Council, and that this has enhanced the prospects for continuing pragmatism in both foreign and domestic policies. Hu and Zhao already play key roles, under Deng, in top-level decision making on foreign as well as domestic policies.

The other two active leaders in the Party's Standing Committee continue to influence foreign policy. Li Xiannian is president of the People's Republic of China and also head of a Central Committee advisory group on foreign policy, which will be discussed later; Chen Yun is China's senior economic planner. But neither of these Party elders participates regularly in the policy deliberations of the Secretariat and State Council, and their roles now appear to be less important in many respects than those of Hu and Zhao.

3.
THE ROLE OF THE POLITBURO

Unlike the Standing Committee, the full Politburo continues to meet occasionally as a group, and it deals with important issues, including foreign policy, but the bulk of available evidence suggests that it is now, as Zhao Ziyang indicates, a "second-line" institution. There is no public record of how often the Politburo meets; only a few of its meetings are publicized. Knowledgeable Chinese state, however, that it generally meets only three to five times a year. Apparently, most of these gatherings are what the Chinese call Enlarged Politburo meetings (to which selected non-Politburo members are invited). These meetings often take place just before Central Committee plenums or Party congresses and before the annual meetings of the National People's Congress (NPC), but some are convened to deal with special problems.

Clearly, when it does meet, the Politburo has the power to make major policy decisions, and on occasion it may still do so.[10] However, there is not a great deal of concrete evidence to indicate that many major foreign policy decisions have emerged from such meetings in recent years, and the infrequency of Politburo meetings doubtless means that many foreign policy decisions are made by others. Considerable evidence suggests that, in reality, some Politburo meetings are now convened primarily to ratify policies already formulated rather than to deliberate on options and make major policy decisions.

The Policy Process: The Establishment of Special Economic Zones

An account of one recent Politburo meeting, contained in an article in the Chinese journal *Liaowang (Outlook)*, which describes the evolution of China's "open door" policy, makes it appear that this particular meeting was primarily to ratify rather than to formulate policy. The article, written by Zeng Jianhui, and entitled "The Birth of an Important Decision—A New Step in Opening the Country to the World," analyzes in great detail the steps leading to the new policy (which clearly is a policy with both foreign and domestic policy aspects of major importance), particularly the decision made (or ratified) by the Politburo, in a meeting on April 30, 1984, to extend to fourteen coastal cities and the island of Hainan some of the special policies applied earlier in four special economic zones.[11] The analysis reveals a great deal about the roles of the major actors in the policy process in China today.

After making the point that, years ago, Deng Xiaoping had emphasized the importance of foreign economic relations to China's overall modernization program, the article asserted that the "strategic principle of opening to the outside world" was decided at the Central Committee's Third Plenum in December 1978.[12]

Thereafter, it said, the Secretariat "deliberated [on] the matter over and over again and unanimously approved the guiding ideology expounded by Comrade Hu Yaobang," which called for use of foreign as well as domestic resources, know-how, and markets. According to the article, the idea of creating "special zones" was first raised by Deng at a central work conference in April 1979, on the basis of suggestions from Xi Zhongxun and Yang Shangkun (both of whom then were Guangdong provincial officials)[13] who argued for "exerting Guangdong's superiority." Presumably, they were pushing for special policies to be applied in their province. (These two men now hold key positions in Peking—Xi as a member of the Party Secretariat and Yang as secretary-general of the Party's Central Military Commission.) Soon thereafter, the plan to establish these zones was "decided upon" by the "Central Committee" (the "Central Committee" may refer in this context to its staff, although the Secretariat as such was not formally re-established until 1980) and by the NPC Standing Committee. The "Central Committee" and the State Council then jointly sent a work team led by Gu Mu (now a key member of both the Party Secretariat and State Council; under the latter he heads a special group in charge of special economic zones) to Guangdong and Fujian to discuss the administration of such zones with provincial officials. In July 1979 the Central Committee and the State Council jointly issued another document establishing four "special zones for export" on a trial basis. This was followed in May 1980 by a joint document naming them "special economic zones." In August 1980 the NPC Standing Committee officially approved the establishment of such zones and formally promulgated regulations for two of them in Guangdong. Then, from 1981 to 1982 the Central Committee (references to the Central

Committee by this time almost certainly mean the Secretariat) and State Council issued three more documents
dealing with the administration of the zones.

The *Liaowang* article conveys the impression that all
the members of the Politburo Standing Committee were
involved in one way or another in formulating the new
policy, and, in certain ways, they doubtless were. It
pointed out that "Hu Yaobang, Ye Jianying, Zhao
Ziyang, Li Xiannian, and other leading comrades" visited the zones where they "conducted investigations" and
gave "on-the-spot guidance." The article did not mention Chen Yun in this context, reporting instead that in
1982 he "gave instructions in a document" that everyone
"should strive to run [the zones] more successfully,"
which seemed to suggest that he was less than totally
enthusiastic about them. In contrast, the article reported
that Hu, during a visit to one of the zones in the spring
of 1983, declared: "You have accomplished the tasks
assigned by the central authorities remarkably." In general, the article indicates that Hu played a key role in
formulating the new policy and was backed by Deng.
The article relates that Deng, who "wanted to personally
witness whether or not the special zones were successful," went in early 1984 with Wang Zhen and Yang
Shangkun to visit three of the zones, after which Deng
"was satisfied with the achievements attained." (Yang's
involvement at this stage was significant because it sym-
bolized the approval—or at least acquiescence—of the
military establishment.)

The *Liaowang* article also outlined the steps that led,
finally, to the decision to open an additional fourteen
coastal cities and Hainan Island. When Deng returned
from his trip south, he convened a forum of "leading
comrades of the central authorities" on February 24,
1984, specifically to discuss the opening of additional

cities as well as how to run the existing zones. At that meeting he reportedly articulated the "guiding ideology . . . to open wide and not to restrict," and he proposed steps to "open some places" and "add some coastal cities" and to apply in the newly opened cities "some policies" already implemented in the special zones. After "heated discussion," the article said, Deng's proposal was approved.

Soon thereafter, the Central Committee and State Council "began to make concrete designs, arrangements, and preparations" for a meeting of representatives from coastal cities to discuss the idea. This forum, jointly convened by the Secretariat and State Council, was held from March 26 to April 6, and was attended by more than ninety people, including representatives from eight coastal cities, Hainan, and the four original zones, and also leaders of the provinces where the cities involved are located, as well as key officials from "the departments concerned of the central authorities." Hu, Zhao, and other Party and state leaders participated, and Deng and Li Xiannian came for what in the West would doubtless be called a "photo opportunity."[14] In the discussions at the forum, the article said, it was agreed that the existing zones all should emulate the most advanced area (Shekou), and representatives from the cities soon to be opened put forth tentative ideas on what they should do. Gu Mu suggested the establishment of study classes in Shanghai and Shenzhen for officials from cities scheduled to be opened. This would enable them to learn from the experience of Shenzhen (one of the existing zones); both Hu Yaobang and Zhao Ziyang discussed Shanghai's special role in carrying out the new policy.

Finally, on April 30, less than a month after this forum, the Politburo held an afternoon meeting in Peking to deal with the question of opening additional cities. Although the article did not use the term, it was an Enlarged Politburo meeting. In addition to regular Politburo members, those attending (as "visitors") included "the leading comrades of the Secretariat of the Chinese Communist Party Central Committee, the State Council, the Central Advisory Commission,[15] and other organs." Remarkably, according to the article, this Politburo meeting was "presided over" by *both* Hu Yaobang and Zhao Ziyang. (Joint chairing of top Party meetings has been reported on a number of occasions since late 1982; it is a major departure from practice in earlier years.)[16] After more "heated discussions," the article said, the meeting "unanimously adopted the minutes of the [March–April] forum" and decided "to further open to the world the fourteen coastal cities" and "to implement in these cities certain policies for special economic zones."

The policy process described in this case is noteworthy in several respects. Deng, as one would expect, played a crucial role. He reportedly initiated certain actions, and when other leaders took the initiative they apparently did so within the general framework already defined by Deng. Moreover, the leadership clearly felt it was essential to associate Deng with every major step in the process.

The Secretariat of the Central Committee (from the time of its reestablishment in 1980) and the State Council, working closely together, appeared to be the key institutions throughout the process. In this instance, Hu and the Secretariat appeared to take the lead. However, the major documents relating to the issue and meetings of major importance were the result of *joint* actions by the Secretariat and State Council; therefore, Zhao, as well as Hu, was directly involved in the critical decisions. (Zhao has been just as strongly committed to the "open door" policy as Hu has been; recently both Hu and Zhao have been vigorous public proponents of it.)[17]

Nearly all top Chinese leaders—especially those on the Standing Committee—were involved in the process in some fashion, in ways that associated them publicly with the policy and indicated their acceptance of it (although in the case of Chen Yun the acceptance seemed to be grudging). The capstone of the process— the Politburo meeting in April—seemed (despite the "heated discussions") in this case to be little more than icing on the cake, a gathering to endorse and ratify the policy. In sum, while several members of the Politburo played important roles, in institutional terms the Secretariat and State Council were most influential in taking the lead and formulating final policy decisions.

The Roles of Individual Politburo Members

Even though the Party Secretariat and State Council appear to have superseded the Politburo and its Standing Committee as China's principal institutions for day-to-day decision making, membership in the latter still represents the pinnacle of status in the Chinese political system, and because the Politburo's members still occupy leadership positions in all important Party and government institutions, as individuals they continue to wield great influence, derived from their status as Politburo members and from their other positions.

The twenty-seven living members of the Twelfth Central Committee's Politburo (twenty-eight were elected, one of whom subsequently died)—who include three alternate members as well as twenty-four regulars—hold key positions in virtually every important political body in China. As noted earlier, of the five active members who are on both the Politburo and its Standing Committee, Hu and Zhao are the two classified as "first line" leaders by virtue of their positions as Party general-secretary and state premier. Deng, though ostensibly now in the "second line," still heads the military commissions in both the Party and government, as well as the Central Advisory Commission established to give honorific positions to retired leaders. The other two active Standing Committee members also hold important institutional posts. Chen Yun heads the Party's Central Commission for Discipline Inspection, and Li Xiannian is president of the People's Republic of China. (Even Ye, though too old to be active, remains, on paper, a vice-chairman of the Military Commission.)

Five members of the Politburo (Wan Li, Xi Zhongxun, Yu Qiuli, and Yao Yilin, as well as Hu Yaobang) belong to the eleven-member Party Secretariat. Two of these plus three other Politburo members belong to the State Council's fifteen-member "inner cabinet" (Wan Li, Yao Yilin, Fang Yi, and Chen Muhua, as well as Zhao Ziyang). Seven Politburo members hold leadership positions in the Party Military Commission. (In addition to Deng and Ye, these include Yang Shangkun, who is permanent vice-chairman and secretary-general; Nie Rongzhen and Xu Xiangqian, two old military marshals who, with Ye, are also vice-chairmen, and Yang Dezhi and Yu Qiuli, two of the four deputy secretaries general.) Other Politburo members holding prestigious institutional positions include Peng Zhen, chairman of the Standing Committee of the NPC; Ulanhu, vice-president of the People's Republic of China; and Deng Yingchao (Zhou Enlai's widow), who heads the Chinese People's Political Consultative Conference (an advisory "united front" body).

Why has the Politburo, whose prestigious membership still makes it the most logical body in many respects for top-level decision making, been eased into the "second line"?

One reason—though not the only one—is that given by Zhao; namely, that "most of the members of the Politburo are aged." As of mid-1984 the average age of the entire membership of the Twelfth Central Committee Politburo was seventy-four.[18] Eight were in their eighties, twelve in their seventies, and six in their sixties—only one was in his fifties. In sum, the Politburo does, as Zhao points out, contain many very old men. Consequently, the shift of decision making to the Secretariat and State Council, where the average age is eight years below the Politburo's, definitely represents a generational, or at least semigenerational, change.[19]

Equally important, the shift undoubtedly has been part of Deng's effort to bypass potential opposition to his policies among Party elders, to help Hu and Zhao play strong leadership roles, and to build up these two men as successors. Deng has tried with some success to change the character of the top leadership by persuading many of China's oldest leaders to accept retirement in return for honorific positions on the Central Advisory Commission, but a number of the old Politburo members have successfully resisted being superannuated. The influence of many of them has been reduced, however, as a result of the shift of decision making to other bodies.

Nevertheless, certain Politburo members who do not belong to either the Secretariat or State Council clearly continue to influence foreign policy. (They engage in a great deal of informal consultation by telephone and in private meetings.) Two of them are particularly important: Li Xiannian and Peng Zhen.

As president of the People's Republic of China, Li Xiannian's principal responsibilities in the field of foreign affairs are mostly ceremonial, but they are not unimportant. According to China's 1982 State Constitution, the president "receives foreign diplomatic representatives on behalf of the People's Republic of China and, in pursuance of decisions of the Standing Committee of the National People's Congress, appoints and recalls plenipotentiary representatives abroad, and ratifies and abrogates treaties and important agreements concluded with foreign states."[20] He also, "in pursuance of decisions of the National People's Congress and its Standing Committee" formally "proclaims a state of war, and issues mobilization orders." In practice, Li, in his position as president, deals with many foreign leaders and diplomats, and as head of state, he, as well as Hu and Zhao, makes important trips abroad. Moreover, because he is a member of the Politburo Standing Committee, his views carry considerable weight on all major issues. Although he is in his mid-seventies, Li is still very vigorous.

Throughout most of his long career, Li's main responsibilities have related to the economy; he has held several ministerial posts dealing with economic affairs, and when he was a vice-premier he had major overall responsibilities for domestic economic policy.[21] However, in recent years, his interests and involvements in foreign affairs appear to have increased. In the early 1980s, in particular, Li's public statements, especially those made in several interviews with foreigners, often were significant indicators of trends in China's foreign policy. Recently, he has made fewer such statements. Nevertheless, his representational role, dealing with foreigners both at home and abroad, has made him a major participant in the conduct of China's foreign relations. In addition, he now chairs an important foreign policy group under the Party Secretariat, which will be discussed below.

Peng Zhen, who chairs the NPC's Standing Committee, also is in a position to exert an influence—personal as well as institutional—on foreign policy deliberations. Constitutionally, the NPC is "the highest organ of state power" in China, and "exercises the legislative power of the state." It has the power "to decide on questions of war and peace." Between the sessions of the full NPC (which is elected for a five-year term and meets once a year), its Standing Committee exercises its powers.

In practice, the NPC has not been a very influential body in most periods in the past, but in recent years it has become more active and vocal. It now has six standing committees, one of which is the Foreign Affairs Committee, headed by Geng Biao, a former minister of national defense and onetime head of the Party's International Liaison Department (the committee's vice-chairmen include Huan Xiang, Fu Hao, Zeng Tao, and Wu Maosun).

From all available evidence, however, even though the NPC, its Standing Committee (which now includes former foreign minister Huang Hua), and its Foreign Affairs Committee are involved to some extent in the foreign policy process, their activities still are not very extensive, and their direct influence is probably still limited (although it is known that on occasion they have raised tough questions with Foreign Ministry officials regarding some issues, including, reportedly, the problem of how to deal with the Taiwan issue). The NPC itself, at its annual plenary meetings, sometimes serves the function of a sounding board for various opinions on policy issues, but there is not much evidence that its discussions have had any great effect on foreign policy. The NPC's Standing Committee is now trying to expand its own international contacts, especially with legislatures in foreign countries. The NPC's Foreign Affairs Committee does meet occasionally and prepares some reports for leading Party and government bodies. Conceivably, these functions, and their significance, may increase in the future. At present, however, these groups do not appear to play primary roles in determining foreign policy.

How much influence Peng Zhen exerts is a subject of debate. There has been some recent speculation among specialists outside of China that his role in the foreign policy area may have been increasing, but there is only very limited evidence to support this. Undoubtedly, Peng exerts a very strong influence in certain policy areas. Even though he is not on the Politburo's Standing Committee, his real status is almost as high as that of Standing Committee members. (Four current members of the Politburo, including Peng, were elected to the Politburo in the 1950s or earlier. Three of the four— Deng, Chen Yun, and Li Xiannian are now on the Standing Committee; only Peng is not.) Peng is still very vigorous, even though he, like Deng and Chen, is in his eighties. His most important policy-making role clearly is in the area of "political-legal affairs."[22] Today, as chairman of the NPC's Standing Committee and head of a special Political and Legal Commission (or Committee) under the Central Committee, he plays a leading role in the drafting of new laws and the development of China's entire legal system (including laws regulating foreign economic relations), in public and state security affairs (including intelligence), and, in fact, in everything relating to "law and order." There is little evidence, however, that he plays any direct role of comparable importance in foreign policy making. Although Peng doubtless exerts a certain influence in this field, he does not appear to be a primary actor in it.

The role of the Politburo member Hu Qiaomu deserves special mention. He, too, is in his eighties and has held important Party posts since pre-1949 revolutionary days. In the 1940s he was secretary to Mao, and he drafted many important documents and commentaries for Mao and the Politburo. In the late 1940s he was appointed head of the New China News Agency (NCNA) and Press Administration; subsequently he became deputy head of the Party's Propaganda Department and deputy secretary general of the Central Committee. In the 1950s Hu helped draft the State Constitution of 1954 and many of the key documents of the Eighth Party Congress in 1956. He also was in charge of editing Mao's selected works and wrote a basic history of the Party.[23]

In recent years Hu has been close to Deng, and in many respects has been the top intellectual-ideological spokesman for many of Deng's policies. He also served as president of the Academy of Social Sciences during its first years, and he again has been given primary responsibilities for editing Mao's works. He has continued to play a major role in drafting key documents relating to both domestic and foreign policy. For example, he was the principal drafter of a 1978 statement ("Act According to Economic Laws . . . ") that put forward many economic reform policies, and he is reported to have had a major role in drafting the foreign policy section (which articulated an "independent foreign policy") of Hu Yaobang's 1982 Party Congress report.

Hu does not appear to be involved in the day-to-day conduct of foreign affairs, or to have any very large influence in the formulation of basic policy. However, apparently he has been involved in drafting some of the most important statements relating to foreign and domestic policy, and, as one informed Chinese puts it:

Hu Qiaomu is definitely involved in the foreign policy process because he is close to Deng and, in many respects, now is China's senior ideological interpreter of current policies, and, even in regard to foreign affairs, it is still necessary for major statements on new positions and policies to be formulated and phrased in ways that are ideologically acceptable.[24]

Hu Qiaomu still plays a significant role in this aspect of the policy process.[25]

As the above discussion indicates, a number of Politburo members exert influence of various kinds on the making of foreign policy in China. However, the bulk of available evidence supports the view that, in institutional terms, the Standing Committee and Politburo, the office of the state president, and the NPC Standing Committee are—in practice if not in theory—in the "second line"; most major foreign policy decisions now appear to emerge from the deliberations of the Party Secretariat and/or State Council (or from informal deliberations involving Deng).

4.
THE PARTY SECRETARIAT AND AFFILIATED GROUPS

THE SECRETARIAT IS DIFFERENT from the Politburo in important respects. It is a smaller group. A larger proportion of its members are specialists or technocrats, directly supervising institutions in their areas of expertise. In addition, the average age of Secretariat members is sixty-six, considerably younger than the average for the Politburo.

The Secretariat meets twice a week—remarkably frequently for a top decision-making group of this kind. It appears, moreover, that it maintains very close liaison with the State Council, the key decision-making body in the government. Not only does Premier Zhao say he participates in Secretariat meetings,[26] three leaders (Wan Li, Yao Yilin, and Gu Mu) are members of both the Secretariat and State Council. As the *Liaowang* article cited earlier indicates, these two bodies often take joint actions and issue joint documents. A great deal of evidence, in sum, corroborates Zhao's statement that the "daily functioning of our government machine rests with the Secretariat and the State Council."

Because the Party apparatus has primacy over government institutions in China, the Party Secretariat clearly is senior to the State Council. As Premier Zhao says, it is the body where "major issues" are decided and to which the State Council refers "issues . . . of great importance."

There is no information available, however, on the amount of time and effort the Secretariat devotes to foreign affairs. Domestic policy issues probably dominate the agendas of its twice-weekly meetings.[27] Nevertheless, it is clear that many of the most important foreign policy matters are referred to and dealt with by this Party body. However, in dealing with such foreign policy issues the Secretariat appears to rely heavily on the advice given both directly and indirectly by members of the State Council, as well as on information and judgments from diverse members of Peking's "foreign affairs community."

Party Secretariat Membership

Because the Secretariat is the top Party body that meets frequently to make policy decisions, it is essential to examine carefully the background of the members of this group. Such an examination reveals that few Secretariat members have extensive knowledge of, or experience in, foreign affairs.[28]

Hu Yaobang himself (aged sixty-nine), who as Party general-secretary heads the Secretariat and formally is the highest-ranking member of the Party (the post of Party chairman held by Mao and Hua Guofeng has been abolished)[29] has spent virtually all of his career in Party work. Over the years, his major leadership responsibilities were in the Young Communist League (YCL)—also called, in English, the Communist Youth League (CYL)—

the Party's youth auxiliary, and in this position he had close ties with Deng, who was Party secretary-general and then general-secretary from the mid-1950s until the late 1960s. (In those years, these posts were not the top ones in the Party, but they were key to running the Party apparatus.) In his position as head of the YCL, Hu traveled abroad a good deal and was actively involved in the international aspects of Party and youth work, but he was not directly involved in diplomatic or other intergovernmental relations. In recent years, prior to assuming his present post, Hu became head of the Organization Department and then head of the Propaganda Department of the Central Committee, and in both these positions he continued to focus his attention mainly on internal Party affairs. Since becoming Party general-secretary, however, Hu has been very active in China's foreign relations. He clearly now is a leader in the foreign affairs field, his knowledge of foreign affairs has rapidly increased, and his role in the conduct of foreign relations is still expanding.

Today, he not only deals with many foreign leaders visiting China, but he has made some very important trips abroad, to non-Communist as well as Communist countries. Some foreign diplomats believe that in relations with certain areas, such as Northeast Asia—including Japan and Korea—Hu rather than Zhao may now play the leading role in managing Chinese relations, while Zhao takes the lead in relations with areas such as Western Europe and North America. Although there is no firm evidence that they have clearly divided their responsibilities in foreign affairs on a geographical basis, the functional division of their primary responsibilities (with Hu focusing on Party affairs and Zhao on governmental functions, both political and economic) does seem to affect the roles they play in the conduct of foreign relations.

Most of the ten other regular and alternate members of the Secretariat (originally there were nine regular members and two alternates, but one regular member has died) have less experience than Hu in foreign affairs, and during the past few years only one has carried major day-to-day responsibilities relating to foreign policy. Four of the Secretariat members have had careers focused mainly on "Party work," dealing with organizational matters, ideology, and propaganda, and today their primary concerns still appear to be in these areas.

Deng Liqun (sixty-nine) has held many posts dealing with student and youth work, ideological and propaganda activities, Party policy research (in Northeast China), and Party journalism (as deputy editor in chief of the Central Committee journal, *Hongqi,* or *Red Flag.*) He also worked for a period of time in the State Council's Policy Research Office, and then was a vice-president of the Academy of Social Sciences. More recently, he has been, successively, deputy director of the Central Committee's General Office and director of the Secretariat's Research Office. He now heads the Central Committee's Propaganda Department.

Xi Zhongxun (seventy-one) also began his career in student work, but then held several political commissar positions in the People's Liberation Army (PLA), followed by numerous organizational posts in both local and central Party organizations. These included positions as deputy head of the Central Committee's Organization Department, Party first secretary in the Northwest, and head of the Central Committee's Propaganda Department. Subsequently, he held several important positions in the government, including the post of secretary-general of the State Council; he also was a vice-premier. Thereafter, he returned to Party work, serving as Party first secretary and governor in Guangdong Province and first political commissar in Guangzhou just prior to his selection as a member of the Secretariat.

Chen Pixian (sixty-eight), like both Hu and Xi, started his career in youth work, then was a Party secretary and political commissar and subsequently held many important local and regional Party positions in Central China, Shanghai, Yunnan, and finally in Hubei, where he was first secretary, just before joining the Secretariat. His career before joining the Secretariat was almost entirely in the provinces. (Some Western analysts believe that Chen, as a Secretariat member, now has certain special responsibilities for dealing with internal security matters and mass organizations, both of which involve some activities relevant to foreign affairs.)

Hu Qili, at fifty-five the youngest full member of the Secretariat (and clearly a rising star in the Party), has had a career that, like Hu Yaobang's, has been mainly in Party work relating to youth. When still very young, he was president of the All-China Students Federation, then a member of the YCL Secretariat. (He had some experience abroad in his youth work, but it was limited.) After serving in several local and regional Party posts in Northeast China, he was appointed vice-president of Qinghua University in Peking, and once again assumed leadership posts in youth organizations, including the YCL and All-China Youth Federation. Finally, just before joining the Secretariat, he held his first important government position as mayor of Tianjin. Recently, he has been director of the Central Committee's General Office, as well as being a Secretariat member. However, during 1984 Wang Zhaoguo replaced Hu Qili as director of the General Office, and Hu became head of the Party Research Office under the Secretariat. Within this office there is a group that deals with foreign affairs, which some observers believe has close relations with, and perhaps even a personnel overlap with, the research staff of the Secretariat's Foreign Affairs Small Group, which will be discussed below. Most important, Hu Qili reportedly now acts as chief of day-to-day Secretariat operations, although he has no formal title indicating this.

These four leaders are notable examples of men who have risen to the top primarily through Party organization work. Although they have broad experience (all having served in a variety of Party positions, and some having held important government positions as well), most of them are notably lacking in experience relating to foreign affairs.

The six other members of the Secretariat represent a different type of leader in China. Although they, too, have been actively involved in Party work (as virtually all China's top leaders have been), their principal responsibilities have been in the government rather than in the Party apparatus, and over time they have become specialists in particular fields. They are representative of China's administrative specialists and technocrats whose roles in the Chinese political system have steadily increased in recent years. Although the main career lines of all six have been in economic work, one now holds a key political-military position (returning to this type of work after more than twenty-five years of economic work), and one, until recently, has headed the Central Committee's department dealing with foreign Communist parties (even though he had no previous foreign affairs experience).

Wan Li (sixty-eight), first vice-premier of the State Council as well as a member of the Secretariat, has held a series of important economic positions in the government. Starting, after 1949, in local posts dealing with finance, construction, and industry in Nanjing and subsequently in Southwest China, Wan Li then moved to

Peking where, at various periods, he was vice-minister of building construction, minister of urban construction, minister of railways, and first vice-minister of light industry. In the late 1950s he was vice-mayor and a Party secretary in Peking. Then, in the immediate post-Mao period, he was Party first secretary in Anhui Province, where he pioneered many agricultural reforms.

Yao Yilin (sixty-seven), the second-ranking vice-premier as well as a member of the Secretariat, also has had a career focusing almost entirely on economic work, mainly finance, trade, and economic planning. Before 1949 he headed the Industry and Commerce Department of the first North China People's Government established by the Communists. After 1949 his posts included those of vice-minister of trade, deputy director of the State Council's Office of Finance and Trade and of the Central Committee's Finance and Trade Department, minister of commerce, first vice-minister of foreign trade, minister of commerce (again), director of the Central Committee's General Office, secretary-general of the State Council's Committee on Financial and Economic Affairs (then headed by Chen Yun), and minister in charge of the State Planning Commission. Yao no longer heads any ministry-level body, but he still plays a significant role in economic affairs. (Some observers believe he frequently represents Chen Yun's cautious views in debates over economic reform; if so, this may also affect his attitudes on issues concerning foreign economic relations.)

Gu Mu (seventy), who in addition to being a Secretariat member is one of the ten State Councillors on the State Council, first achieved prominence in regional Party and governmental posts, but then became—like Wan and Yao—an economic administrator or technocrat, dealing with industry, transportation, capital construction, and foreign trade and investment. After serving as mayor, Party secretary, and political commissar in Jinan (Shandong Province), he became deputy secretary of the Shanghai Party Committee. Thereafter, he held a series of major governmental positions in Peking dealing with the economy: vice-minister of the State Capital Construction Commission, deputy director of the State Council's Third Staff Office (which dealt with heavy industry, construction, and planning), vice-minister of the State Economic Commission, minister of the State Capital Construction Commission, and, finally, minister of both the State Import and Export Commission and the State Foreign Investment Control Commission (at that time he also was a vice-premier). Today, he holds no ministerial post but continues to have a significant influence in the areas of his expertise.

Yu Qiuli (seventy) began his career in political-military affairs and then for a quarter century concentrated on economic affairs, but has now returned to political-military affairs. Immediately after 1949 Yu held a series of commissar and training posts in the PLA, but then, still in the army, he moved into financial and logistical work. From the late 1950s on, however, he held major government positions dealing with economic matters, as minister of the Ministry of Petroleum Industry, then minister of the State Planning Commission, and subsequently head of the State Energy Commission. (He was a key member of the "petroleum faction.") Currently, he again holds a key political-military position in the PLA, as head of its General Political Department. (He also is a deputy secretary general of the Military Commission.) Yu is the only representative of the PLA on the Secretariat at present.

(The twelfth member of the Secretariat, Yang Yong, who has died, was the only military officer on the

Secretariat who had held command positions throughout most of his career; he had been not only deputy
commander and commander of the Chinese forces in
Korea, commander in the Peking area, and commander
in Xinjiang Province, but also deputy chief of the General Staff Department and a deputy secretary general of
the Military Commission.)

The two alternate members of the Secretariat are
Qiao Shi and Hao Jianxiu. Qiao (sixty) headed the
Central Committee's International Liaison Department
until recently, and he was the one Secretariat member
with major, specialized responsibilities for foreign affairs. However, this department deals primarily with
Party rather than government relations abroad, and
Qiao's most important previous position had no relationship to foreign affairs. Before coming to Peking, he had
spent years in the steel industry, first as head of a section
of the Anshan Iron and Steel Company, then as chief of
the design institute and subsequently of the research
institute of the Jiuquan Iron and Steel Company. He is a
notable example of China's group of rising technocrats.
(Recently, Qiao has become head of the Party's Organization Department; the new head of the International
Liaison Department is Qian Liren, who for years had
been in youth work, closely associated with Hu Yaobang,
and then was a deputy head of the International Liaison
Department for some time before succeeding Qiao as its
head. Qian's foreign affairs experience in Party relations
abroad has been substantial.)

Hao Jianxiu (forty-nine), a woman and by far the
youngest member of the Secretariat, is another good
example of China's younger technocrats. Starting as a
worker in a textile plant in Qingdao (Shandong), she
became a technician and then a deputy director of a
plant. She then held several posts in the city Party

Committee, trade union organizations, and local government; she also was president of the city's women's federation and held provincial leadership posts in both the trade union and women's organization. These positions were a springboard from which she rose to important positions in Peking, as vice-minister and then minister of the Textile Industry Ministry (and vice-president of the All-China's Women's Federation).

As the above data show, the careers of some of these economic administrators and technocrats on the Secretariat have included certain kinds of experience relevant to foreign affairs. For example, Gu Mu, Yao Yilin, and Yu Qiuli all have dealt with China's foreign economic relations. As noted, Qiao Shi's responsibilities as head of the International Relations Department concerned the Party's foreign relations, and his successor has had considerable experience in Party relations abroad. Since becoming first vice-premier, Wan Li also has been increasingly involved in foreign affairs. Yet it is clear that the expertise in foreign relations of most Secretariat members is limited, and not one Secretariat member has been concerned mainly with government foreign policy or diplomacy through his or her career. It is obvious, therefore, that when dealing with foreign policy issues the members of the Secretariat rely heavily on information, analyses, and judgments from others who have greater experience and expertise in this field.

Several groups under the Secretariat perform this function. The Central Committee bureaucracy run by the Secretariat is extensive and includes a sizable number of departments, committees, small groups, and research units, all presumably coordinated by the Central Committee's General Office. No complete table of organization of this apparatus is available, but there is some information available on certain parts of the apparatus. (During the Cultural Revolution the Secretariat stopped functioning and many Central Committee departments were dismantled or became inactive. The rebuilding of the apparatus since then has been gradual.)

Both the Organization Department and Propaganda Department, which deal with personnel, ideology, training, indoctrination, and the entire range of Party organizational affairs, have always been powerful bodies in the Party apparatus, and they remain so today. At various periods in the past, the Party apparatus also has included numerous departments and/or other organizational units dealing with economic affairs, paralleling comparable bodies in the government structure. Precisely what organs now exist within the Party to deal with the entire range of economic affairs is not entirely clear. Undoubtedly, as in the past, there again are units that supervise the implementation of Party policies by government bodies in all economic fields, but less is known now about such units than was the case before the Cultural Revolution. The Central Committee also has a variety of units dealing with political-legal affairs, cultural affairs, and the media. In addition, there are several units that have important roles in China's foreign policy–making process.

Foreign Affairs Small Group

It now appears that the most important group under the Secretariat that deals broadly with foreign policy is the Foreign Affairs Small Group (Waishi Xiaozu).

Until recently, this group had never been discussed publicly by the Chinese, but Premier Zhao, when asked in the already cited July 1984 interview, about what organizations are involved in the process of foreign policy making in China, stated: "In foreign affairs, there is a Foreign Affairs Small Group in our Party. All organizations concerned with foreign affairs participate in this group." He then indicated that it is essentially an advisory rather than a decision-making body. "The principal function of the Foreign Affairs Small Group," he said, "is to exchange views, to study problems, and to communicate." It does "not decide what concrete measures are to be taken."[30]

This group apparently is the one body that meets fairly frequently and assembles key Party and governmental leaders and other experts most directly responsible for and best informed about the conduct of foreign policy specifically for the purpose of advising the Secretariat. Knowledgeable Chinese say that, on occasion, it has met as often as once a week—although there is no regular schedule for its meetings, and it probably meets less frequently than this under normal circumstances. It is chaired, Chinese foreign policy experts say, by President Li Xiannian, and its core membership includes: Premier Zhao; First Vice-premier Wan Li; former foreign minister Ji Pengfei, who is the state councillor responsible for coordinating foreign policy; the present Foreign Minister Wu Xueqian; and Minister of Foreign Economic Relations and Trade Chen Muhua. The head of the Party's International Liaison Department sometimes participates, but it is unclear whether or not he is a core member. (The head of the International Liaison Department and other key Party and government officials concerned with foreign affairs are also reported to sit in on some meetings of the Secretariat itself, even though they may not be members of it.) According to some reports, the Foreign Affairs Small Group has its own research staff.

One striking thing about the core membership of the group is that it is composed entirely of key *government* leaders dealing with foreign affairs. (It is noteworthy, also, that the core membership does not, apparently, include any active military leaders.) Equally important, the Foreign Affairs Small Group invites to its meetings many other specialists on foreign affairs from throughout Peking's foreign affairs community. Chinese specialists who have taken part in such meetings say that the choice of participants depends on the meeting's agenda, and individuals invited to attend include not only working-level specialists from the Party and Foreign Ministry and other government organizations but also influential retired diplomats and academic specialists from both government research institutes and the Academy of Social Sciences' units.[31] The size of the meetings varies, but they are reported to be small enough to permit real discussion. Some who have participated in the group's meetings state that Li Xiannian does not dominate but rather acts as a fairly permissive "chairman of the board." Even though the group is not a decision-making body, it does produce analyses and recommendations that can and do affect policy decisions. The group not only provides a vital channel for the views of China's foreign affairs experts to reach the Secretariat, it is a key link between the Secretariat and the principal government leaders in charge of the conduct of foreign relations. According to some Chinese, it also has a role in monitoring policy implementation.

There have been comparable but by no means identical small groups in China dealing with foreign affairs in the past. For example, some years ago published Chinese sources referred to a group in the early 1960s (under the International Liaison Office, which later became a department) that included Wang Jiaxiang and was said to have discussed the possibility of adopting a new foreign policy based on "three reconciliations and one reduction."[32] Wang Jiaxiang also headed a small group dealing with foreign affairs (called the Central Group for Studying Foreign Policy) under Zhou Enlai in the early 1970s. It appears, however, that because the present group draws broadly on the expertise of the entire foreign policy community in Peking, it may be different in significant respects from comparable bodies in the past.

International Liaison Department

Another important group under the Secretariat that deals with certain aspects of foreign affairs is the already-mentioned International Liaison Department (Guoji Lianluo Bu). Until recently, little could be learned about this department from published Chinese sources. (There was, in fact, no mention of it in the Chinese press during the 1950s and 1960s; the little that was learned about it at that time came mainly from the East European press.)[33] Nevertheless, Chinese acknowledge that it has long been a major department under the Central Committee, with primary responsibility for relations with other Communist parties, and now some of its activities are described in the Chinese press. It has been headed by a number of individuals who have played significant roles in China's foreign relations, including Ji Pengfei and Geng Biao. Some of its deputy directors also have played important foreign policy roles. One of these is Wu Xiuquan, one of a group of Chinese generals who, following the Communist takeover in 1949, moved from military to foreign policy posts; the main focus of Wu's subsequent foreign affairs career was on China's relations with Communist bloc countries, and this, not surprisingly, seems to have been true of many who have been key figures in the department. China's present foreign minister, Wu Xueqian, also once served as deputy director of the department. Although the department's recent head, Qiao Shi, had relatively little foreign affairs experience, the current head, Qian Liren, has—as noted earlier—long been involved in the Party's foreign relations.

It is not entirely clear to what extent the International Liaison Department may be directly involved, together with the Foreign Ministry, in intergovernmental relations with other Communist-ruled nations. Strictly speaking, governmental relations are the responsibility of the Foreign Ministry, yet it appears that on occasion the line between Party-to-Party and state-to-state relations may be blurred, and in some intergovernmental relationships (probably including, for example, China's relations with North Korea), both the International Liaison Department and the Foreign Ministry seem to play significant roles.

In one respect, the International Liaison Department has been given a wider mandate in recent years. It now not only maintains ties with foreign Communist parties but is also developing contacts with socialist, social democratic, and labor parties, as well as varied political parties in Third World nations; it also provides support to Chinese mass organizations that develop relationships with foreign labor, women's, youth, and student organizations.[34] Hu Yaobang's expanding role in foreign relations also has resulted in increasing activity by the department in some areas, such as relations with Korea.

However, it appears that the functions of the International Liaison Department have changed somewhat over time. China does not now have Party-to-Party relations with the Soviet Union, which formerly was one of the department's most important foci of activity, and the Foreign Ministry is in charge of governmental ties with Moscow. Moreover, since the 1970s the Chinese have reduced, and played down, their support of Communist parties engaged in revolutionary struggles, and the earlier concept of a community of Communist parties and governments no longer underlies Chinese policies in the way it once did. Nevertheless, this department obviously continues to play a very significant role in policy toward other Communist countries and in developing ties with both Communist and non-Communist parties in many countries.

Many other Central Committee units under the Secretariat doubtless play secondary roles in shaping China's foreign relations. The United Front Work Department (Tongzhan Gongzuo Bu), another regular and long-standing Party department, is responsible for dealings with non-Communist Chinese groups, some aspects of which have foreign policy implications—for example, in regard to the Overseas Chinese. The Propaganda Department (Xuanchuan Bu), also is involved to some extent in foreign policy–related matters; it has a News Bureau (Xinwen Ju) that is usually headed by a leading journalist, which concerns itself with the international as well as domestic activities of journalistic organizations such as the *People's Daily (Renmin Ribao)* and New China News Agency (Xinhua She), which themselves influence the making of foreign policy in ways that will be described later. There is also, under the Central Committee, a Foreign Propaganda Small Group (Duiwai Xuanchuan Xiaozu), which is a coordinating body for all informational and propaganda activities abroad. According to some Chinese sources, there also is a Central Committee small group that coordinates all "cultural affairs," including activities abroad as well as at home. None of these, however, is believed to play any very significant role either in the general formulation of foreign policy or in decision making on major specific issues; they are primarily involved in policy implementation.

5.
THE STATE COUNCIL

In the Chinese system the Secretariat, as a Party decision-making body, enjoys a position superior to that of the State Council, and the Party clearly has primacy in determining overall policy and in supervising foreign relations in the broadest sense (including Party-to-Party ties, people-to-people links, propaganda abroad, and basic military-strategic decisions, as well as government-to-government ties). However, it is the State Council and the government ministries under it that are responsible for the daily conduct of government-to-government foreign relations. Zhao states that, while the Party decides "major issues," the State Council is in charge of "routine work" and decides "concrete" issues, but these distinctions are not clear-cut.[35] Many policy decisions on secondary issues obviously are made by the State Council—in fact, many implementing decisions are made by the Foreign Ministry and other organs that are subordinate to the State Council. General foreign policy guidelines, and the overall framework for policy, are defined by the Party and/or by Deng Xiaoping, as well as by the State Council itself, but the "routine work" and "concrete

51

issues" to which Zhao refers include many if not most matters that arise in day-to-day intergovernmental relations. (Chinese foreign affairs experts stress that the policy-making process is more highly concentrated in the field of foreign policy than in other fields, and that, therefore, the authority of the State Council to make policy decisions in this field is more limited than in many other fields; but, in making this point, they seem to be referring mainly to broad, "basic" policies with which Deng and the Secretariat deal.)

Constitutionally, as was noted earlier, the National People's Congress (or, between its annual sessions, its Standing Committee) is the "highest organ of state power" in China, and the State Council is its "executive body" and "the highest organ of state administration." In practice, the State Council manages most domestic and foreign governmental affairs, and for the most part it does so within overall policy guidelines defined by the Party rather than by the NPC (even though, gradually, the NPC is playing an increasing role in lawmaking, if not in policy-making). In foreign policy, although the president of the People's Republic of China and the NPC do play certain roles—which were briefly described earlier—they are quite limited, and the State Council is by far the most important government body involved in both the making and implementation of foreign policy.

The full State Council, which has more than fifty members, including the premier, vice-premiers, state councillors, and heads of all ministries and commissions (there are forty-five ministry-level organs), is far too large a body, however, to be an effective decision-making organ. According to informed Chinese, it meets fairly infrequently—sometimes only about once a quarter, at most no more than once a month—and its meetings appear to be convened mainly for the purpose of briefing all the ministers on important developments and policy decisions already made.

The key day-to-day decision-making body in the government is the "inner cabinet" of the State Council, a fifteen-member group consisting of the premier, four vice-premiers, and ten state councillors, seven of whom concurrently head important ministries or commissions.[36] (The post of state councillor is a relatively new one, established when the number of vice-premiers was cut, and most of the state councillors bear special responsibilities, of the sort formerly carried by vice-premiers, for work in specified areas.) Like the Party Secretariat, this State Council group (hereafter referred to simply as the "inner cabinet") meets regularly, and frequently—twice a week, according to Premier Zhao.

When Premier Zhao stated in his already-cited interview that the "daily functioning" of the political system in China is in the hands of both the State Council and the Secretariat, he added: "The State Council [by which he meant the 'inner cabinet'] meets twice a week. That is to say, it holds regular meetings. These correspond to cabinet meetings in foreign countries. Problems that various ministries cannot solve themselves are put forward to be discussed at these meetings."[37] Zhao pointed out that, in addition to the vice-premiers, the state councillors who attend these meetings include "the foreign minister, the minister of defense, the minister of foreign economic relations and trade, the minister of finance, and the chairman of the State Planning Commission." (Zhao could have added the ministers in charge of the State Scientific and Technological Commission and the State Economic Commission. It may be more than coincidence that these men he failed to mention were replaced in the fall of 1984.)

Zhao chairs the twice-weekly meetings of this group and is reported to play a strong leadership role in it.

"These meetings," he himself pointed out, "are presided over by the premier, that is to say, by me. We practice a system of 'responsibility by the premier.' " However, the other members of the group all have major responsibilities. Each vice-premier and state councillor has one or more special areas of functional responsibility, in many cases covering the work of several ministries and other organizations.

The membership of the State Council's "inner cabinet," even more than that of the Party Secretariat, symbolizes the change in the character of the leadership that has been occurring in China.[38] As in the case of the Secretariat, the average age of the "inner cabinet" now (as of mid-1984) is sixty-six. Moreover, although it still has four members in their seventies, eight (the majority) of its members are in their sixties, and three are in their fifties; it seems likely that all or most of the elder members will gradually be replaced by younger men. Earlier, it was noted that about half of the members of the Party Secretariat symbolize the recent trend toward technocratic expertise. The membership of the "inner cabinet" is by far the best illustration of this trend; it is overwhelmingly technocratic in the sense that virtually every member is a specialist with long administrative or technical experience in a particular area of government work. The careers of a majority have focused on economic affairs. However, in contrast to the Secretariat's relative lack of expertise directly related to foreign policy, the "inner cabinet" includes the top government leaders who are operationally responsible for overall foreign policy, economic policy abroad, and national defense, and many of its other members are ministers who manage economic bureaucracies that are increasingly involved in various ways in China's expanding foreign relations. Because the "inner cabinet" is responsible for the entire range of the government's activities, it is probable that problems of economic development and reform usually dominate its agenda; nevertheless, a majority of the most important foreign policy issues concerning intergovernmental relations undoubtedly are discussed by this body, and, on many issues, this probably is where policy decisions are made. An examination of the careers of its members (as of mid-1984) indicates that, as a group, they have considerably more experience relevant to foreign policy making than does the membership of the Secretariat, even though, not surprisingly, only a few of them are really foreign affairs professionals.

The Premier

In the Deng-Hu-Zhao triumvirate, Premier Zhao is the one most directly and extensively involved in the actual day-to-day governance of China, including the conduct of foreign affairs. As in the case of Hu Yaobang, Zhao's experience in foreign affairs was limited before 1980, but since becoming premier he has been deeply involved in all aspects of China's foreign relations and has rapidly acquired expertise and experience in this field.

Zhao rose in the Party hierarchy through a succession of important provincial posts. While still in his early thirties, he led the land reform program in Guangdong Province, rising thereafter to become Party first secretary in the province. Years later, after a brief period as a Party secretary in Inner Mongolia, he returned to Guangdong where he again became first secretary. Then, in 1975, he was appointed first secretary in China's largest province, Sichuan; it was his performance there that led Deng to back him for the premiership. In Sichuan, Zhao not only coped successfully with a very difficult political and economic situation during the post-Mao transition, but he was a pioneer (as Wan Li was in Anhui) in devising—flexibly and innovatively—agricultural and other reform policies that later served as models on the national level.

Chinese assert that when Zhao was in Guangdong—a province with broader external contacts than most provinces—he acquired some experience relevant to foreign affairs; in fact, however, throughout his career, his concerns were primarily domestic, so that when he assumed the premiership he had little real expertise on foreign policy (this is true, of course, of many government leaders who rise to similar positions in other countries), and at first he appeared somewhat uncertain about (and may, in fact, have been fairly uninvolved with) foreign policy issues. Nevertheless, since 1981–82 he has been deeply and continuously involved in China's foreign policy and has made several important state visits abroad. Over time, Zhao has shown an increasing sophistication and skill in dealing with foreign affairs, and he now projects the image of a leader who is quite confident about his ability to handle China's international relations.

Vice-premiers

None of the four men who now are vice-premiers has had a career focusing primarily on foreign affairs; all four are economic specialists. However, three of the four have been involved in China's foreign economic relations, and their responsibilities now compel them to concern themselves with this and other aspects of foreign affairs.

The career of Wan Li (sixty-eight), first vice-premier and one of the three men who belong to both the

Secretariat and State Council, was described earlier. Since his experience in Anhui, he has had special responsibility concerning agricultural policy, and this still seems to be the case. However, as first vice-premier (he is acting premier when Zhao is absent), he must concern himself, across the board, with all government functions, including foreign policy, and, as noted earlier, he, as well as Zhao, is a core member of the Party's Foreign Affairs Small Group.

The career of Yao Yilin (sixty-seven)—the second-ranking vice-premier and another individual belonging to both the Secretariat and State Council—also was discussed earlier. As was noted, he has long been involved in planning, foreign trade, and other economic activities and, in his economic posts, has had a good deal of experience very relevant to foreign economic policy.

The two newest vice-premiers, appointed in 1983, are both in their fifties, and they are dramatic symbols of generational change and the trend toward technocracy in the Chinese leadership.

Li Peng (fifty-six), a native of Deng Xiaoping's home province, Sichuan, is an engineer and energy expert. Li is reported to have been the son of a revolutionary hero and to have been raised by Zhou Enlai and Deng Yingchao. Starting his career as an electricity technician in North China, he studied at the Moscow Power Institute in the late 1940s. Thereafter, he held a series of posts in the electric power industry in Northeast China, including those of chief engineer of one major power station, then director of another, and subsequently deputy chief engineer of the Electric Power Administration of the entire region. From there he moved to join Peking's Power Supply Bureau, ultimately becoming its head. Thereafter, he was deputy secretary of the Party Committee of the Peking Electric Power Administration

and then the administration's director. From this springboard, he rose to be minister of power industry and then
vice-minister of water conservancy and electric power.
Today, he has special responsibility for supervising the
energy field (though Kang Shi'en, an oil expert, apparently continues to share some of this responsibility).
Because of the increasing involvement of foreign oil
companies and international organizations in China's
energy development, Li is very actively involved in
certain aspects of China's foreign economic relations.

Tian Jiyun (fifty-five), the other recently appointed
vice-premier, has had a career focusing on finance,
trade, and economic planning. Starting as a confidential
secretary to a financial official in Southwest China, he
became an instructor in a Guizhou Province training
center for financial cadres. Thereafter, he worked his
way up the ladder in the economic field in Guizhou,
ultimately becoming deputy director of the provincial
Department of Finance. After moving to Sichuan, he
rose to become director of the Department of Finance—
in the province where Zhao Ziyang was in charge. It is
believed that Hu Yaobang personally selected him to be
China's youngest vice-premier. Reportedly, Tian continues to have special responsibilities related to finance.
Until 1984 there was little indication that he had involved himself in foreign affairs, but the fact that recently he was sent on an African tour may indicate that
top leaders are now deliberately encouraging him to
acquire some experience abroad.

State Councillors

Of the ten state councillors on the "inner cabinet,"
three are senior leaders who formerly headed ministries

but no longer hold ministerial posts; however, they continue to have special responsibilities in their fields of expertise.

One of these, Ji Pengfei (seventy-four), is responsible under the State Council for overall coordination of foreign affairs. Ji belonged to the group of revolutionary generals who were converted to diplomats immediately after the Communist takeover in 1949. From the time of his appointment as chief of mission—with ambassadorial rank—to East Germany in 1950, Ji's entire career has been in foreign affairs. From Germany he returned to the Foreign Ministry and rose to be vice foreign minister, and then, some years later, foreign minister. Subsequently, he headed the Central Committee's International Liaison Department for a period of time. His role in coordinating foreign affairs obviously is important, as will be described below.

The career of Gu Mu (seventy), the third person (besides Wan Li and Yao Yilin) who serves on both the Secretariat and State Council, was also described earlier. His ministerial posts in the 1950s and 1960s were concerned with investment and heavy industry and involved him deeply in China's foreign economic relations—in the 1950s, mainly relations with the Soviet Union. The ministerial posts he last held, in which he was directly responsible for control of imports, exports, and foreign investment, placed him in charge of major aspects of China's economic relations with Japan and Western nations. Gu now heads a small group under the State Council in charge of the special economic zones, where China's economic interactions with the outside world are most intense.

The other state councillor without any ministerial portfolio at present is Kang Shi'en (sixty-nine), who was for years a key leader in China's petroleum development.

From the 1950s on, he was continuously involved in China's energy relations with the outside world. After serving as military representative at a major oil field in Northwest China, Kang became director of the Northwest Petroleum Administration, then head of the Peking General Petroleum Administration, after which he rose steadily, becoming, successively, first vice-minister of the Ministry of Petroleum Industry and then head of the Ministry of Petroleum and Chemical Industries, vice-premier, minister of the State Economic Commission, vice-minister of the State Energy Commission, and, finally, head of the Ministry of Petroleum Industry. Subsequently, after an offshore-rig disaster, as well as a decline in the power of the so-called petroleum faction (which was said to have included Li Xiannian and Yu Qiuli), Kang lost influence, although he still plays a role of some importance in the energy field. (However, it is reported that Kang now has serious health problems and could be replaced before too long.)

The other seven state councillors all head key ministries. Three of them are of particular importance in relation to foreign affairs. Wu Xueqian (sixty-three) is China's foreign minister and heads the ministry most directly involved in the conduct of foreign affairs. Wu spent the early part of his career mainly in student and Young Communist League (YCL) work, much like Hu Yaobang, with whom Wu has developed a close relationship over the years. At that time, he did not have a great deal of involvement in foreign affairs except in the context of Party work; however, he did serve as head of the YCL's International Liaison Department. Subsequently, he was a director of a bureau under the Central Committee's International Liaison Department and then became a deputy director of the department before becoming, first, vice-minister and finally minister of the Ministry of Foreign Affairs. Western diplomats had little contact with Wu before he became foreign minister, but since then many have judged him to be very effective and professional in his dealings with them. (According to some reports, Wu may soon be replaced as foreign minister; if so, it is believed he is likely to move up rather than out.)

Chen Muhua (sixty-three), the minister of the Ministry of Foreign Economic Relations and Trade (MOFERT), has spent her entire career working in China's economic bureaucracies, dealing mainly with foreign economic relations. Starting, after 1949, as a division chief in the State Planning Commission, she subsequently worked in the unit dealing with imports of complete plants in the General Bureau for Economic Relations with Foreign Countries, becoming a bureau chief after this body was made a ministry-level commission. Subsequently, she rose to be the minister of the Commission for Economic Relations with Foreign Countries, and, finally, was made head of the Ministry of Foreign Economic Relations and Trade. Because of the huge size and broad foreign economic responsibilities of this ministry, its head is a key individual in the foreign affairs field, and Chen meets regularly, as will be noted below, with State Councillor Ji and Foreign Minister Wu to deal with foreign policy issues. (Some observers, both Chinese and foreign, speculate that a stronger individual may soon be appointed to this position.)

Zhang Aiping (seventy-four), who heads the Ministry of National Defense, is the one state councillor who has been a professional military man throughout his career. A participant in the Long March in the 1930s, Zhang held a succession of leadership posts in the PLA, mainly as a military commander although occasionally as a political commissar. After rising to be deputy chief of staff, his subsequent positions focused on economic, scientific, and technical matters relating to the military establishment, and just before his appointment as minister of national defense he served as deputy director of the Office of National Defense Industries and then as head of the PLA's Science and Technology Commission for National Defense, at which time he also was a vice-premier. As will be discussed later, Zhang is not directly involved in the State Council's special group responsible for coordination of foreign affairs. This is surprising in many respects, since the PLA obviously has strong interests and concerns relating to foreign policy, and the role of China's military establishment obviously is of critical importance to Chinese thinking about foreign affairs. Nevertheless, there is little doubt that Zhang, as the only real military professional now directly representing the PLA on either the Secretariat or State Council, has an important influence on some aspects of foreign policy (although some observers believe his concerns focus on issues relating to the military budget, technology transfers, and military modernization more than on broad foreign policy issues). (Because Zhang is frail, he could soon be replaced by a younger man, but it seems likely that whoever is minister of national defense will be a state councillor and play a comparable role.)

The four remaining state councillors (as of mid-1984) head China's top government bodies in the fields of economic planning, finance, and science and technology; all of them now have certain responsibilities that relate to China's foreign economic relations.

Song Ping (sixty-seven) is chairman of the State Planning Commission, responsible for long-term economic plans. Song began his career in positions that related to Party training, research, ideology, and propaganda. Then he worked for the New China News

Agency. In the immediate postwar years, he was a political secretary to Zhou Enlai. Then, after 1949, he moved to Northeast China and soon became involved in trade-union work. This led to his appointment as director of the State Planning Commission's Labor and Wages Planning Bureau, after which he rose to be vice-minister of labor and then vice-minister of the State Planning Commission. Subsequently, he held important regional Party posts as first secretary, first political commissar, and chairman of the Revolutionary Committee in Gansu Province; but he returned to Peking to become first vice-minister of the State Planning Commission and, finally, its minister.

Zhang Jingfu (seventy), the head of the State Economic Commission until recently (the fall of 1984), was responsible for implementing economic plans. Earlier in his career, after holding several commissar positions in the PLA and then a number of regional Party and government posts (including those of vice-mayor of Hangzhou and director of the Zhejiang Province Financial and Economic Affairs Committee), Zhang's entire subsequent career was in organizations concerned with economic, scientific, and technical affairs. After serving as vice-minister of local industry, he became vice-minister of the State Scientific and Technological Commission and vice-president of the Chinese Academy of Sciences. In the mid-1970s he headed the Ministry of Finance. Subsequently, he spent a period of time as Party first secretary and governor of Anhui Province before becoming minister of the State Economic Commission.[39]

Wang Bingqian (fifty-nine), minister of finance, has been involved in financial affairs ever since the 1940s, when he held minor posts in financial organs in Central Hebei District and then in the Communists' North China People's Government. His career from 1949 on is a striking illustration of the way in which some technical experts have risen in the system. Wang worked his way gradually from the bottom to the top of the Ministry of Finance, serving, successively, as a section head, a division head, deputy director and then director of a department, vice-minister, and finally minister.

Fang Yi (sixty-eight) immediately after 1949 held a number of important Party and government posts in Fujian Province and then Shanghai. In Shanghai he began his longtime involvement in economic, scientific, and technical affairs. He rose to be head of the Shanghai Committee on Financial and Economic Affairs and then moved to Peking, where he became, successively, vice-minister of the Ministry of Finance, vice-minister of the State Planning Commission, minister of the Commission for Economic Relations with Foreign Countries, president of the Academy of Sciences, and finally minister of the State Scientific and Technological Commission until the fall of 1984 (and also, for a time, vice-premier). Fang's career has involved him extensively in foreign economic relations, especially in the field of science and technology.[40]

This "inner cabinet" group of fifteen leaders is a strong body, well qualified to deal collectively with all major policy problems, including foreign policy issues, facing the Chinese government. Because the group includes not only the heads of the most important ministries directly concerned with foreign affairs but also those in charge of other key economic ministries and commissions that increasingly have become involved in China's foreign relations, its membership, taken together, is more competent to address most foreign policy issues than any other top group in either the Party or government, and because it meets twice a week, it has ample opportunity to discuss such issues.

Coordination Point for Foreign Policy

One of the State Council's basic problems in dealing with all policy areas is how to coordinate effectively the activities of the numerous government ministries, commissions, and other organizations operating in particular fields. Ever since the establishment of their first central government in 1949, Chinese leaders have experimented with a variety of coordinating mechanisms. Since then, there always have been, under the top executive body in the government, a number of offices or groups responsible for supervising specified functional areas of government work (usually there have been parallel or comparable bodies within the Party, under the Central Committee, coordinating the same areas). The areas into which work has been functionally divided have been based on what the Chinese call "systems" (*xitong*), each of which includes all institutions doing related work, at all levels, from the center to local areas.

During the first years of the regime, there were five committees under the Government Administration Council—the equivalent of today's State Council—which covered culture and education; finance and economics; political and legal affairs; people's supervision; and planning.[41] It is not clear that any committee for foreign affairs was established at that time; perhaps Zhou Enlai— who was both premier and foreign minister—simply coordinated this field from his own staff office.

In 1954, when the State Council was established, a number of State Council "staff offices" (*bangongshi*) were set up. Headed by strong leaders, they had sizable staffs and are said to have exercised considerable authority, on behalf of the State Council, in supervising all subordinate bodies. Eight such staff offices, identified by number, were first established in 1954. The eight were: 1st, public security, internal affairs, justice, "supervision," and labor; 2nd, culture, education, and science; 3rd, heavy industry, construction, and planning; 4th, light industry; 5th, finance, trade, and food; 6th, transport and communications; 7th, agriculture, forestry, and conservation; and 8th, "united front" work. Formal government tables still did not list any staff office for foreign affairs.

Finally, in 1958, when Zhou Enlai handed over leadership of the Foreign Ministry to Chen Yi, a special staff office for foreign affairs was listed in formal tables of organization, and it was headed by Foreign Minister Chen Yi.[42] (From 1959 on, all such staff offices were referred to by name rather than number. Over time there were some organizational changes; however, from 1959 until the Cultural Revolution the major staff offices were for foreign affairs; agriculture and forestry; culture and education; finance and trade; industry and communication; and political and legal affairs—at times called internal affairs.)[43]

These staff offices stopped functioning during the Cultural Revolution and were never revived in their original form. However, not surprisingly, new mechanisms have since evolved to cope with the problem of coordination. Although information about these is still limited, on the basis of what is now known about them they appear to have less power than the old staff offices did, but it is clear that they serve important—in fact essential—coordinating functions. Today, these coordinating points no longer are labeled "staff offices"; they are now simply called *kou*. (Literally translated, *kou* means a mouth or opening, but in this context it is best translated as "channel." In discussing functional groups of institutions and mechanisms for coordinating them, Chinese now use the term *"guei kou,"* which means to bring together various units under one *kou*. Because the responsibility of each *kou* is to coordinate a specified area of work, I will henceforth refer to a *kou* simply as a "coordination point.")

It is difficult to obtain any clear picture of the overall structure of coordination points under the State Council. In general, however, it appears that most functional "systems," as traditionally defined by the Chinese, have designated coordination points, and that the most important ones are probably headed at least by state councillors, if not by vice-premiers.

State Councillor Ji Pengfei (a former foreign minister) heads the foreign affairs coordination point *(waishi kou)*. In this position, he has certain responsibilities covering the gamut of foreign affairs *(waishi)*. (In Chinese, the term *waijiao*, or "foreign policy," refers primarily to the intergovernmental, diplomatic aspects of foreign relations; *waishi* is a broader term, covering all aspects of foreign affairs.) However, Ji is reported to have only a small staff, so there is some doubt about his office's ability—or mandate—to coordinate closely the myriad activities of all the ministries and other agencies, including "mass" organizations, involved in the conduct of China's foreign affairs. His primary responsibility seems to be one of high-level coordination of diplomatic-political and economic policy—which requires, above all, coordination between the Foreign Ministry and the Ministry of Foreign Economic Relations and Trade.

According to Premier Zhao, "those who are in charge of foreign affairs [under the State Council] include Ji Pengfei, Wu Xueqian, both state councillors, and also the minister of foreign economic relations and trade, Chen Muhua. These three persons meet frequently to discuss foreign affairs and communicate among themselves. When there are problems that they cannot solve, they raise them with the State Council." (It is noteworthy, as stated earlier, that the minister of national defense is not a member of this group—one of many indications, to be discussed later, that the defense establishment and civilian agencies involved in foreign affairs operate fairly autonomously, for the most part, below the very top level of the leadership. In the United States, the defense secretary probably would belong to any comparable coordinating group.) The triumvirate of Ji, Wu, and Chen deals with a broad range of political-diplomatic and economic issues, sometimes making decisions and sometimes preparing position papers and recommendations that go to the State Council for consideration. Ji also has other special responsibilities, for example, as head of the special State Council small group handling Hong Kong affairs.

Other Coordinating Mechanisms

Ji's group is the most important but not the only government mechanism below the State Council–level in charge of coordinating foreign affairs activities. The premier's and the State Council's own staffs—or at least certain individuals on these staffs—participate actively in many deliberations on foreign policy issues. For example, Chen Chu—a deputy secretary general of the State Council (and a former Chinese ambassador to the United Nations)—is said to have been involved in the drafting of Hu Yaobang's first public statement (at the Twelfth Party Congress) on China's "independent foreign policy."

There are also ministry-level commissions and certain ministries with broad coordinating responsibilities, especially in regard to economic plans and policies. In particular, the State Planning Commission, the State Economic Commission, and the Ministry of Finance play major coordinating roles that affect foreign relations as well as domestic policy. In addition, some ministries have established bilateral groups whose task is to coordinate policies. For example, the Foreign Ministry and the Ministry of Foreign Economic Relations and Trade (MOFERT) do not simply rely on the meetings of Ji's group to deal with problems of coordination. According to a vice-minister of MOFERT, the ministers and all vice-ministers of these two ministries meet at least every two months or so, and more frequently if necessary, to deal with common concerns; on major issues, they sometimes submit joint reports to the State Council for its consideration.[44]

The problems of lateral communication and coordination are complicated in any complex bureaucratic system, and they are especially difficult in China because of the stress on vertical hierarchy. Some Chinese and many foreign observers emphasize the weakness of lateral communication and coordination at the working levels of China's bureaucracies, in foreign affairs as in other fields. However, in interviews, lower-level Chinese officials maintain that there are more extensive informal as well as formal contacts among ministries at various levels—including the "bureau" or "desk" levels—than is sometimes assumed by outside observers. The foreign affairs bureaus or offices that are part of the structure of virtually all ministries—and many other institutions in China—play a role in interagency coordination (as well as in managing contacts with foreigners), but many contacts, according to working-level officials, take place directly (through telephone calls, personal contacts, and ad hoc meetings) between bureaus or desk officers dealing with interrelated problems in different ministries.

In the Chinese government, as in most governments, ad hoc interagency groups are established, when necessary, to coordinate the work of different ministries on particular problems. In China, however, these appear to operate somewhat differently from those in countries such as the United States. According to informed Chinese, when there is a need for a special group to coordinate the work of two or more ministries on a particular issue, the ministry bearing the "principal responsibility" for the activity involved generally takes the initiative in establishing such a group, and although the representatives of other ministries involved can express their views freely, their roles are essentially advisory, and the convening ministry is ultimately responsible for whatever recommendations or decisions emerge. Apparently there is no requirement, as there is in some comparable U.S. interagency groups, to produce a consensus position that represents a compromise among the views of the agencies involved.

The various groups—permanent and ad hoc—engaged in coordination tasks within the Chinese system sometimes make definite decisions, but often, as is true in other systems, they simply prepare data or recommendations that are passed up the line to higher decision-making bodies. Senior officials in China's foreign affairs apparatus describe a hierarchy of decision-making levels at which foreign policy issues can be considered and coordination of policy discussed. When a particular ministry is unable itself to make a decision because an issue involves other ministries, there is likely to be direct, informal discussion with members of the other ministry or ministries involved. If informal discussion does not resolve the issue, an interagency group may be set up on the initiative of the ministry with primary responsibility for the problem. If the issue requires higher-level consideration, it then may be considered by Ji Pengfei's group. If it is sufficiently important, it will then be considered by the State Council's "inner cabinet." Some key issues in this latter category are then considered by the Party, and often these are first discussed by the Foreign Affairs Small Group under the Party Secretariat. Really "major" broad issues are then considered by the Secretariat itself. Finally, some of the most important issues go directly to Deng Xiaoping.

This schematic portrayal obviously does not describe a process that is followed in any rigid way. Decision making is never so orderly or systematic in any system. Some decisions are made at lower levels, while others are made at the top of the hierarchy without such systematic deliberation at all lower levels. Members of the Foreign Ministry sometimes express frustration, moreover, about insufficient coordination between their institution and other key ministries—especially the Defense Ministry, but even some major economic ministries—on foreign policy issues. Nevertheless, the available evidence suggests that the decision-making process is more systematic and orderly than in the past, and that coordination of the many participants in the process is improving.

Except for foreign policy issues of such importance that they require consideration by the Party Secretariat, or Deng himself, the State Council is normally the highest decision-making or coordinating level. Bodies at lower levels in the government structure provide it with the data, analyses, and recommendations required for its members to make decisions. The character of the State Council's membership, and the fact that it meets twice weekly, enables it to deal effectively with a great many issues.

State Council Research Coordination

The State Council obtains information and analyses on foreign affairs from numerous sources, including all the ministries in addition to coordinating bodies already mentioned. These sources also include many ad hoc groups established to deal with special problems. Some examples are those under Gu Mu and Ji Pengfei, dealing, specifically, with special economic zones and Hong Kong, but there are many more. The State Council also draws widely upon the expertise of the foreign affairs research establishment, which will be discussed later.

Recently, also, several high-level research centers have been established directly under the State Council to mobilize expertise for research on priority issues and to coordinate the Chinese research establishment's contribution to the decision-making process. There are now at least five of these, dealing with broad economic research, technology, prices, and law, in addition to foreign policy. Although these centers do not "control" the scattered members of the research establishment in their particular fields, they are authorized to ask experts—wherever they are located—to work on key policy problems and to prepare background studies and policy recommendations. Some of these new centers are well-established, strong organizations—a good example is the Economic Research Center, which is said to have fifty to sixty staff members, including many of China's leading economists.

The research center that has been established to perform this function in the foreign affairs field is the Center of International Studies (Guoji Wenti Yanjiu Zhongxin, which, translated literally, means International Studies Research Center). It is relatively new and still small, having fewer than a dozen full-time staff members. However, it can be expected to become increasingly important over time.

This center is headed by Huan Xiang, one of the most respected of China's retired diplomats and academic specialists on foreign affairs, who is an active and influential advisor in foreign affairs. Huan started his career as a journalist, then served in several important diplomatic and Foreign Ministry posts. He was, for example, director of the West European and African Department in the Foreign Ministry in the 1950s and then Chinese chargé d'affaires in London with ambassadorial rank before Sino-British relations were raised to the ambassadorial level. In the 1960s he was an assistant to the foreign minister, a position now labeled assistant foreign minister, which ranks just below that of vice foreign minister. In the post-Mao period, he was appointed ambassador to Belgium and the European Economic Community. Subsequently, he became a vice-president of the newly established Academy of Social Sciences, where he took the lead in developing the academy's research and exchanges relating to international affairs; he still is one of the academy's senior advisors. In his present position, even though his research center is still small and therefore cannot closely coordinate all foreign affairs research (most background papers and analyses on foreign policy prepared by research organizations in the international relations field still go directly to top decision-making bodies and leaders, rather than through his center), it plays a role of growing importance, and he and his staff sometimes review, and add their comments to, reports prepared for top leaders by other research institutions. Huan is a frequent participant in the Party's Foreign Affairs Small Group (and is reported to have close ties with its staff), and he frequently writes authoritative articles on foreign policy. He clearly plays a very influential personal role in the system, and he has direct access to China's top government and Party leaders.

6.
THE FOREIGN MINISTRY

Wᴡᴀᴛ ʜᴀꜱ ʙᴇᴇɴ ᴅᴇꜱᴄʀɪʙᴇᴅ so far is the decision-making superstructure for foreign policy in China. The actual day-to-day conduct of foreign relations is largely in the hands of ministries under the State Council, of which the Ministry of Foreign Affairs is the most important. Even though Premier Zhao labels the Foreign Ministry as an "implementing body," carrying out policies defined by higher authorities, in China, as elsewhere, the line between making and implementing foreign policy is not always clear. Leading members of the Foreign Ministry not only recommend policy to others, but they themselves participate in decision making at higher levels. Moreover, both the Foreign Ministry's staff and its diplomats abroad help to shape policy, to a certain extent, in the course of their day-to-day operations.

The Foreign Ministry in China has undergone considerable change over time; gradually its personnel has become more experienced and expert, and the ministry has adjusted its structure to deal with the broadening range of complex foreign policy issues with which China

75

has had to deal. Headed by Premier Zhou Enlai from 1949 to 1958, and then by Chen Yi until the Cultural Revolution, it has always been regarded as one of the country's senior ministries, as comparable ministries generally are in other countries. During the Cultural Revolution, however, it was highly politicized, and for a period of time, when radical leaders seized control of it, it hardly functioned at all. Starting in the early 1970s (especially since 1976), it has been steadily strengthened. It has had four foreign ministers during this period—Ji Pengfei, Qiao Guanhua, Huang Hua, and Wu Xueqian. Even though none of these has enjoyed the status or power of the men who occupied this position before the Cultural Revolution, the ministry's responsibilities have steadily increased in response to China's expanding foreign relations. Whoever the foreign minister is, he plays a key role in foreign policy making.

The trend during the past few years in the Foreign Ministry, as in most of China's top government bodies, has been toward steadily increasing professionalism; the structure of the ministry has been adapted gradually to meet new needs; and its operations have been rationalized to improve the ministry's effectiveness. Recently, a major effort has been made to appoint younger people with demonstrated professional competence to responsible positions.

The top leaders in the Foreign Ministry (as of mid-1984) consist of the foreign minister, five vice-ministers, three assistant ministers, and one formally designated advisor (though there have been some changes since then). Of the vice-ministers, one, Yao Guang, is a full member of the Party Central Committee; two, Qian Qichen and Han Xu, are alternate members; and the other two, Gong Dafei and Wen Yezhan, are senior diplomats.[45] The assistant ministers, Zhou Nan,

Liu Shuqing, and Zhu Qizhen, rank just below the vice-ministers and they are slated soon to become vice-ministers.[46] The one designated advisor is a retired senior diplomat, Han Nianlong, who once was a vice-minister and now heads an organization, closely affiliated with the ministry, involved in international exchanges. These ten men constitute a top-level policy group within the ministry, and they meet regularly (although Han Nianlong states that he does not attend all such meetings). According to some well-informed Chinese, this policy group normally meets about twice a week to discuss major foreign policy issues. (Foreign Minister Wu also heads the "leading members small group," or Party "fraction," which is the top Party group within the ministry, appointed by the Central Committee.)

Each vice-minister and assistant minister carries special responsibility for one or more specified areas of Foreign Ministry work. For example, Qian Qichen is primarily responsible for dealing with the Soviet Union and Eastern Europe. He holds periodic meetings with both Soviet Vice Foreign Minister M. S. Kapitsa, to discuss broad international issues, and Leonid F. Ilyichev, to discuss bilateral issues. Vice Foreign Minister Han Xu was formerly deputy head (with the rank of ambassador) of the Chinese diplomatic mission in Washington, and was chief of protocol in the ministry, and then headed the ministry's Department of American and Oceanian Affairs. Since becoming vice foreign minister, he has had overall responsibility for China's relations with the Americas as well as for two functional areas— treaties and protocol.[47] Assistant Foreign Minister Zhu Qizhen, who succeeded Han as head of the department dealing with the Americas and Oceania, is in direct charge of relations with the United States.[48]

Under the top ministry leadership, there are twelve major departments *(si)*, six of which have regional/ geographic responsibilities and six of which have responsibilities for functional areas. The six regional departments cover (1) American and Oceanian affairs; (2) Asian affairs (both Japan and the Asian Communist nations are included here); (3) Asian-African affairs (the Middle East and North Africa); (4) African affairs (sub-Saharan Africa); (5) Soviet and East European affairs; and (6) West European affairs. The six functional departments deal with (1) international affairs (this is sometimes referred to as international organizations and conferences affairs); (2) international laws and treaties affairs; (3) information (the ministry spokesman belongs to this department); (4) consular affairs; (5) protocol; and (6) administration. Below the departments are divisions *(chu)*, which are the operating "desks." For example, under the Department of American and Oceanian Affairs, one division deals with U.S. affairs.

At the top level of the ministry there is a small research group—usually headed by a very senior diplomat—which serves the ministry's leaders. Called the Foreign Policy Research Office (Waijiao Zhengce Yanjiushi), it is small—with ten to twenty staff members, according to individuals who work for it—and it concentrates on producing studies on important issues that deal with international problems that transcend bilateral relationships or regional boundaries.

It is at the level of the country desks in the Chinese Foreign Ministry, as in comparable bodies elsewhere, that much of the day-to-day activity involved in the conduct of foreign policy takes place. These divisions vary in size and importance. The desk dealing with U.S. affairs has about twenty staff members. Of these, according to its director, roughly two-thirds, or about thirteen or fourteen people, are engaged in "operational" tasks,

while about a third—six or seven—are engaged in research and analysis directly related to immediate policy
problems.

To deal with China's relations with any particular
country, therefore, there normally are, in the ministry's
hierarchy, a vice foreign minister with overall regional
responsibility (and sometimes also an assistant foreign
minister dealing with the area), a department head
dealing with the region in which the country is located,
and a division ("desk") head in charge of country affairs.
In the area of China's relations with the United States,
Vice Foreign Minister Han Xu has been the top responsible official; he has a staff of his own, although he says it
is very small. Under him, Zhu Qizhen, as assistant
minister (until his recent promotion) and head of the
Department of American and Oceanian Affairs, has had
specific responsibility for the region that includes the
United States, Canada, Central and Latin America, and
Australia and New Zealand; Zhu also has his own staff.
(He has recently been promoted to vice foreign minister.) Then, at the level of the U.S. desk, which currently
(as of mid-1984) is headed by Wang Li, there is, as
already stated, a staff of about twenty. One measure of
the trend toward professionalism—and specialization—
in the ministry is the fact that most of these people have
had considerable experience in U.S. affairs; a sizable
number of them have been stationed in official posts in
Washington; and a few, including the desk head, have
spent time in U.S. academic institutions (at The Johns
Hopkins School of Advanced International Studies
[SAIS], in Wang's case).

As the Chinese government has faced new kinds of
foreign policy problems in recent years, it has taken
some steps to develop new, specialized groups to handle
them. One example is in the field of arms control (or, to

use the terminology preferred by the Chinese, "disarmament"). Until quite recently, even though Chinese leaders often have issued broad statements on arms control issues, China has not been very deeply involved itself in international discussions of issues in this field. Now that it is a more active participant in arms control discussions, especially in Geneva, the Foreign Ministry has begun to develop a few specialists to deal with this field. Although there still is nothing in the Chinese system comparable to the U.S. Arms Control and Disarmament Agency, the first step toward developing a specialized unit to deal with these issues has been the establishment, within the Foreign Ministry, of a small group of a half dozen or so arms control specialists, under the ministry's International Affairs Department, to do detailed research and analysis on arms control issues. There also are a few individuals elsewhere in the Chinese system who work on these issues—some in the military establishment, others scattered in research organizations. The ministry's own research institute (to be discussed later) has a few, and the Institute of (North) American Studies of the Academy of Social Sciences also is developing a section that deals with strategic problems, including related arms control issues. Some of the individuals in the small community of scholars conversant with arms control issues now are knowledgeable about thinking in the West and U.S.S.R. on the subject; a few have spent time at U.S. research programs dealing with arms control such as those at the Rand Corporation and Stanford University. However, these beginnings are still small.

Actually, to a Western observer, one notable fact is the apparent lack of any sizable specialized functional units within the Foreign Ministry to deal with certain important aspects of foreign policy making. If one compares the Chinese Foreign Ministry with the U.S. Department of

State, for example, one is struck by the seeming absence of equivalents to several units that are important in the U.S. structure. There are, for example, no real equivalents of the State Department's Bureau of Intelligence and Research, Bureau of Economic and Business Affairs, or Bureau of Politico-Military Affairs. The functions performed by these units in the State Department are performed in one way or another in the Chinese system, but they are performed differently (and appear to be given less emphasis than in the United States). Information and analyses are provided to policymakers from varied sources, a process that will be discussed in greater detail later. Some groups have also been set up to coordinate military as well as economic policy with the political-diplomatic aspects of foreign policy; these, too, will be discussed below. But without well-developed, specialized units to address these matters within the Foreign Ministry, Chinese policymakers are probably limited in their ability to coordinate these many aspects of foreign policy effectively. Within the ministry, one consequence is that very broad responsibilities are assigned to the country desks, which must deal with the entire range of foreign policy issues with only limited support from well-developed, specialized, in-house units dealing with information (intelligence) and analysis, economic affairs, and political-military affairs.

In China's numerous embassies abroad (Peking now has diplomatic relations with more than 120 countries), many staff members working on specialized areas are drawn from ministries other than the Foreign Ministry. The National Defense Ministry and the General Staff Department provide military attachés, the Ministry of Foreign Economic Relations and Trade provides commercial officers, the Ministry of Education and the Ministry of Culture provide personnel for exchange programs, and so on. According to Chinese diplomats, such embassy personnel are under "dual leadership," that is, they report both to their own ministry and to the Foreign Ministry. The leadership principle in Chinese embassies, as described by Chinese diplomats, sounds similar in some respects to the American organizational concept, which specifies that an embassy's staff should be a "country team" with the ambassador clearly in charge. It also appears that Chinese ambassadors have at least as much difficulty as American diplomats do in translating this concept into reality—that is, in ensuring effective coordination of staff members with differing concerns, responsible to different ministries.

Sources of Information and Analysis

Information and analyses for policymakers in the Foreign Ministry (and Party and government bodies above it) come from various sources. According to senior ministry officials, the most important sources include reports from Chinese embassies and other missions abroad; a daily compilation of materials from foreign publications called *Reference Materials (Cankao Ziliao)*, published by the New China News Agency (NCNA); in-house research produced within the ministry; the analyses of a research institute directly affiliated with the ministry; the analyses produced by other research institutes; and studies or information coming from other academic and journalistic sources.

Obviously, the reporting from diplomats abroad is important. There is no basis, however, for outsiders to judge its quantity or other characteristics. Also important is the ministry's in-house research and analysis which, as already stated, is done by its small, top-level policy research body and at the desk level. However, because this is limited in quantity, the ministry's top policymakers rely a great deal on information and analysis from both journalistic sources and research institutions; these appear to play an even more important role in the Chinese system than they do in the United States.

Particularly important in China is the daily publication entitled *Reference Materials,* issued by NCNA. This is a classified *(neibu)* daily compilation of news and articles from foreign newspapers and journals around the world. It is quite comprehensive and includes a wide range of articles, some of them critical of China and Chinese policies. Two issues of *Reference Materials* appear daily, in printed form, each normally averaging 40 to 50 pages (but at times as many as 80 to 100 pages). In addition, a daily, four-page digest of major world developments accompanies *Reference Materials.* Although the circulation of *Reference Materials* is quite restricted, at least compared to most Chinese publications, it is sent free through organizational channels to top Chinese leaders and policymakers concerned with foreign affairs who have a "need to know" what the world's press is reporting. (Also included are a few analytical articles by NCNA correspondents abroad.) The exact circulation of *Reference Materials* is unknown but is reported to be in the thousands. (Informed Chinese sources estimate its circulation is "several thousand.")

This publication is of special importance in China because it is a major source of information on world affairs not only for Foreign Ministry officials but for the leadership as a whole. On the surface, it appears to be similar in some respects to the daily output of the Foreign Broadcast Information Service (FBIS) in the United States. Yet, there is a big difference. While FBIS materials are read mainly by specialists and researchers in the United States, *Reference Materials* goes to all top leaders and policymakers, and, according to informed Chinese, it is one of their primary sources for information on world affairs. What this means is that "raw" information from the foreign press, as contrasted with "processed," evaluated intelligence and analysis, plays a greater role in informing China's foreign policymakers than it does in the United States. Obviously, top Chinese leaders and policymakers do not have time to read the two large daily issues of *Reference Materials* in their entirety. However, according to senior Chinese officials, almost everyone concerned with foreign affairs at least reads the four-page summary as well as selected articles that are brought to their attention by subordinates and staff members. (The role of personal secretaries and other staff members obviously is significant in this respect, since they influence what senior officials choose to read.) In the Foreign Ministry, top leaders reportedly read a considerable amount of the daily output of *Reference Materials,* while working-level officials read all that relates directly to their areas of responsibility.

For background analyses of foreign affairs, Chinese leaders and policy-making officials rely to a considerable extent on studies produced by both government and academic research institutions. For the Foreign Ministry, the most important of these is its own Institute of International Studies, which, although labeled "independent," is closely affiliated with the ministry and is staffed to a large extent by ex-diplomats and former ministry employees. (There are many transfers of personnel, back and forth, between the ministry and the institute.) The institute produces the kind of policy-related reports that, in the United States, would be written largely by in-house research units; it therefore is, in some respects, the functional equivalent of the Department of State's Bureau of Intelligence and Research. Some of its studies are commissioned by leaders and working-level officials in the ministry—or are requested by leaders of other institutions—while some are done on its own initiative. (Recently, staff members say, more studies are done on their own initiative than in response to outside requests.) The "consumers" of the institute's output are not limited to personnel in the Foreign Ministry; their studies and reports circulate throughout the official foreign affairs community and the leadership. Moreover, the ministry does not rely solely on its own institute for research and analysis. It can and does request—and in many cases obtains without requesting—studies produced by other research institutes dealing with a wide range of foreign policy issues. In short, the entire research establishment serves the entire leadership and all bureaucracies concerned with foreign policy. As will be discussed later, moreover, not only is the research establishment expanding, but it appears to be undergoing a steady professionalization, in part because China's research institutes have developed increasing contacts with foreign research organizations and many of their staff members have had increasing experience abroad.

Personnel—Sources and Characteristics

The trend toward professionalism also is apparent in the ministry's personnel policies and training efforts. As noted earlier, the ministry is now trying to appoint younger and better-trained individuals to key positions at all levels. It has also started to develop new procedures and policies for work evaluation and promotion (though apparently it still has a considerable way to go to do what is needed in this area). It has sent an increasing number of persons abroad for study, and it has taken steps to improve its own training program.

The ministry has its own Foreign Affairs College (Waijiao Xueyuan, also translated as "Foreign Affairs Academy"), which has a long history. It was established in 1955, closed in 1966, reopened in 1973, and has been given increased support since 1980. Recently, it has provided a majority of entry-level recruits for the diplomatic service and ministry. Until very recently, the college's main program was a two- or three-year postgraduate course, almost all the graduates of which were hired by the Foreign Ministry. In addition, it had shorter training courses for recruits hired directly from foreign language institutes or universities. Since 1980 it also has had a five-year undergraduate program; its first class is soon to graduate. Total student enrollment now stands at roughly 400, with about 200 in the undergraduate program, more than 60 in the graduate program, and the rest in advanced postgraduate programs or mid-career training classes. The college is trying to strengthen both its faculty and curriculum. A few junior faculty members have been sent to study at institutions abroad (including, in the United States, The Johns Hopkins School of Advanced International Studies and the Fletcher School of Law and Diplomacy at Tufts University). A few foreign scholars—so far mainly language teachers—have been invited to teach at the college. There have even been discussions about possible exchanges between the college and the U.S. State Department's Foreign Service Institute. In developing its curriculum, moreover, the college is now placing more emphasis on substantive courses on foreign affairs (in the past, knowledge of a foreign language was usually regarded as the most essential prerequisite for entry-level jobs in the field of foreign affairs).[49]

Over time, the sources for and characteristics of personnel in the Foreign Ministry have undergone change. Although there is not enough biographical data on ministry or foreign service personnel to make any detailed analysis, it is possible to identify certain important changes in the sources for personnel; these have affected not only the ministry but other institutions that are actively involved in foreign affairs.

Many of China's senior foreign affairs specialists belong to several categories of personnel recruited in the early days of the Communist regime. One of these groups consists of men whom Zhou Enlai gathered around him when he was the Communists' wartime negotiator and contact man with foreign diplomats and newsmen in Chongqing during the Sino-Japanese War. Many of these were very young when Zhou recruited them; quite a few were just out of university, some were young journalists. Many came from two universities in particular—especially Yanjing University at first; later St. John's University provided sizable numbers. Many of these early recruits worked for NCNA. A few of them worked directly under Zhou throughout much of the 1940s and 1950s and participated in all or most of the key events in China's foreign relations at that time, including the Communists' negotiations with the Nationalists and Americans right after World War II, the truce talks and political negotiations at Panmunjom in Korea, and the Geneva and Bandung conferences in 1954–55.[50] Some of the senior members of this group rose to the very top of the Foreign Ministry. For example, Qiao Guanhua and Huang Hua both rose to become foreign minister. Others, including Wang Bingnan, Chen Jiakang, Pu Shouchang, and Zhang Hanfu became vice foreign ministers. Many of the oldest members of this group have died or been superannuated. Some, such as

Wang Bingnan, however, continue to be senior advisors. Though nearing retirement, others have continued to be active diplomats and have been very important actors in the making of Chinese foreign policy. For example, Zhang Wenjin (who was close to Zhou from at least the early 1950s onward) played a key role in the 1970s at every stage in the development of Sino-American relations, from the time of Kissinger's 1971 trip through the negotiations for normalization of diplomatic relations in 1978. In 1978 he and Han Nianlong were the two Chinese professionals who participated, with Deng Xiaoping, in the final negotiations. (After serving as a vice foreign minister for several years, Zhang Wenjin was then appointed ambassador to the United States but is scheduled to return to Peking in 1985.)

In addition, many of the youngest members of the group Zhou recruited in the 1940s and early 1950s (who mainly served as secretaries and speechwriters at the start) are still very actively involved in the foreign affairs community in Peking or abroad. Some, such as Han Xu, still occupy high positions in the Foreign Ministry (Han is reported to be replacing Zhang Wenjin in Washington in 1985). Others, such as Ji Chaozhu and Zhang Zai hold second-level posts in embassies abroad. (Harvard educated Ji returned to China at the time of the Communist takeover and, like many others, began his career in foreign affairs at Panmunjom; he is now a minister-counselor in the Chinese embassy in Washington. Zhang left Peking University before graduation on the eve of the Communist takeover in 1949, then returned to join the Foreign Ministry staff in 1950. He too is a minister-counselor in Washington.) A number of others now occupy important positions in journalistic and academic institutions. For example, Li Shenzhi is director of the Institute of (North) American Studies, and Pu Shan is director of the Institute of World Economy and Politics in the Academy of Social Sciences. (Pu Shan is a brother of Pu Shouchang, and both attended Harvard.) Close personal ties link many of them. For example, Vice Foreign Minister Han Xu, Li Shenzhi, Peng Di (until recently head of the NCNA bureau in Washington), and one of the top editors dealing with international news at the *People's Daily,* all were not only college mates but classmates in the Yanjing University campus in Sichuan during the Sino-Japanese War.

Another important group that dates to the early days of the Communist regime comprises revolutionary generals recruited right after 1949 to be ambassadors. State Councillor Ji Pengfei is a good example. Many have held numerous diplomatic and Foreign Ministry posts ever since then, although they, too, like the senior members of the group most closely linked to Zhou, are now gradually passing from the scene.

It is not entirely clear if there is an identifiable group in the Chinese foreign affairs community composed of men who, by virtue of their training in the Soviet Union in the 1950s, have special ties among themselves. There is some evidence, however, that such a group does exist (Soviet-trained men certainly occupy important posts in many economic ministries) and that its members hold key positions in the Foreign Ministry and abroad dealing with Soviet and East European affairs; many men from this group are still in their fifties.

Starting in the 1950s, younger people were recruited into the Foreign Ministry from major new sources (as well as from other foreign affairs institutions)—namely, China's educational system and, in particular, the Foreign Ministry's own college (which has already been discussed), and the foreign language institutions established at the time. Because, as mentioned earlier, knowledge of foreign languages was regarded as one of the most important requirements for dealing with foreign affairs, many new recruits for many types of jobs in the foreign affairs community came from the Peking Foreign Languages Institute and comparable institutes elsewhere. Ever since the 1950s, graduates of these institutes (which, while stressing language study, also give a few substantive courses relating to foreign affairs) have contributed staff to the foreign affairs bureaus and offices that major ministries and many other institutions in China have established. Graduates of these foreign language institutes also are employed by the journalistic and "mass" organizations involved in China's foreign relations, and some have joined the Foreign Ministry. Graduates of these institutes often have started as interpreters or translators and have then gone on to more substantive work.

The foreign language institutes continue to provide many junior personnel for foreign affairs work, but the Foreign Ministry and other institutions increasingly are recognizing the need for people with training that goes well beyond the study of languages. As a result, the majority of junior personnel are now being drawn from specialized foreign affairs training organizations such as the ministry's own college—and from those major universities that are now trying to develop or strengthen programs in international relations and foreign area studies. Some other organizations also have important specialized training institutions. For example, there is in Peking a College of International Relations (Guoji Guanxi Xueyuan), founded under its present title in 1965, closed during the Cultural Revolution, and then reopened in 1978. It is closely linked to the Institute of Contemporary International Relations (Xiandai Guoji Guanxi Yanjiusuo)—discussed later—and, according to some Chinese, it has one of the strongest international relations programs in China, including a four-year undergraduate program and a two-year graduate program. There also is a College of International Politics (Guoji Zhengzhi Xueyuan), established in Peking in 1978, which is quite large, with nearly 600 students. At least until recently, it has been under the Ministry of Public Security, but it probably has been shifted to the new Ministry of State Security in the course of a bureaucratic reorganization that took place during 1982–83—which also will be discussed later.

The trend toward increased professionalism among China's foreign affairs specialists has manifested itself in many ways. For foreigners who have dealt with Chinese diplomats both before and after the country's shift toward pragmatism in the late 1970s, one particularly striking change has been a dramatic decline in the use of ideological rhetoric and in the kind of simplistic formulas that in earlier years dominated many Chinese discussions of foreign policy issues. Chinese diplomats now stress the need for sophistication and realism rather than sloganeering in dealing with complex international problems.

It is difficult to judge, however, to what extent political and ideological constraints still may work against the trend toward professionalism. The Party organization departments (with lower-level units linked to the Central Committee's Organization Department) have always played a crucial role in determining personnel assignments in the government, as in other institutions; they doubtless still do, even though personnel criteria are changing. In addition, Party units are still embedded at all levels within the Foreign Ministry, as well as all other ministries. In addition to the Party "fraction" (*dang zu,* also referred to as "leading Party members group") at the top, which, undoubtedly, is still the ultimate authority within the ministry, there is a Ministry Party Committee supervising Party branches at lower levels; all Party members in the ministry must belong to the branches and participate in "Party life" (including study and other meetings). All top leaders in the ministry are Party members; reportedly, everyone from the level of the first secretary—or equivalent—up must belong to the Party.

Moreover, during 1984, foreign affairs institutions in Peking were required to take an active part in the Party's "rectification" campaign (a three-year program), and they had to devote a considerable amount of time to rectification meetings.

Both the regular activities of Party organizations, which of necessity concern issues of Party discipline and ideological matters, and the special indoctrination efforts associated with rectification meetings, could work against the trend toward professionalism, at least to some extent. Yet a good deal of evidence suggests that, as the ethos of professionalism has been strengthened, the impact of Party meetings on professional work has declined, and that, while the Party structure and forms remain, the influence of the Party on substantive policy matters has diminished. The rectification campaign appears to have had only a minor impact on the regular work of Peking's foreign affairs specialists, and probably it has not slowed the trend toward professionalism very much, if at all. Actually, in recent rectification meetings the Party itself has stressed the need for greater professionalization.

However, one cannot yet say that there has been a clear, permanent victory of pragmatism and professionalism over ideology and politics; it remains to be seen whether present trends toward professionalism will continue indefinitely, and, if so, how far they will go.

7.
ECONOMIC, MILITARY, AND CULTURAL INSTITUTIONS

Ministry of Foreign Economic Relations and Trade

IN CHINESE EYES, clearly the second most important ministry directly involved in the day-to-day conduct of foreign policy is the Ministry of Foreign Economic Relations and Trade (MOFERT). As China's foreign economic relations have broadened, economic issues have become increasingly salient. Because of this, a special effort has been made, as indicated earlier, to coordinate foreign economic policy with diplomatic-political policy, both through Ji Pengfei's coordinating group and through the regular bilateral meetings of Foreign Ministry and MOFERT ministers and vice-ministers. However, because MOFERT is such a huge institution with such broad responsibilities (and perhaps also because the Foreign Ministry lacks anything like a bureau of economic affairs), the coordination is far from perfect; in many respects, the Foreign Ministry seems to play a secondary role in shaping China's foreign economic policy.

MOFERT was established in 1982 through a merger of four ministry-level bodies—the Ministry of Foreign

Trade, the Ministry of Foreign Economic Relations (responsible for China's foreign aid), the State Import and Export Commission, and the State Foreign Investment Control Commission. Its present responsibilities are therefore enormous. It concentrates in one body functions that in the United States are widely dispersed in the Commerce Department, the Agency for International Development, the State Department's Bureau of Economic and Business Affairs, and a great many other federal departments and agencies.

According to Jia Shi, a senior vice-minister of MOFERT, the ministry is "responsible for the study and implementation of foreign economic and trade policies, for the administration of foreign trade matters, for laws and regulations on foreign economic relations, and for coordination of activities relating to foreign economic relations."[51] He maintains that MOFERT not only coordinates its work closely with the State Planning Commission and other top economic planning bodies but that it also has "very close relations" and "very good coordination" with the Foreign Ministry. In fact, he stresses the importance of meshing foreign economic policy with overall foreign policy. MOFERT's economic policies, he says, "support overall foreign policy needs," and are "closely coordinated with foreign policy needs." It does "not make decisions solely on the basis of the economic benefit or the needs of specific enterprises," he says, " but on the basis of overall foreign policy needs." (To support this, he cites examples of decisions that, he says, were shaped by political instead of strictly economic considerations.) "These kinds of decisions," according to Jia, "are made by both the Foreign Ministry and this ministry"; however, he stresses that MOFERT rather than the Foreign Ministry is primarily responsible for China's foreign economic relations, and it appears that, in reality, while foreign economic policy clearly conforms to broad guidelines laid down by the Foreign Ministry and higher authorities, a great many decisions are made by MOFERT with only minor participation from the Foreign Ministry. It is not very clear, moreover, exactly how MOFERT's policies are coordinated on a day-to-day basis with the many other economic ministries and agencies involved in China's foreign relations—including not only the State Planning Commission and State Economic Commission but also the State Scientific and Technological Commission, the National Defense Commission for Science, Technology, and Industry, the Finance Ministry, the People's Bank and its affiliates, and many others. (Probably, however, a good deal of coordination occurs in contacts between personnel at the department and bureau levels.)

What is clear is that MOFERT is a powerful ministry with a broad mandate, and that it now plays a large role in China's conduct of foreign relations and in influencing foreign policy. Under MOFERT's top leadership, which consists (as of mid-1984) of the minister, four vice-ministers, three assistant ministers, and several advisors (a group that, as in the case of the comparable group in the Foreign Ministry, is the ministry's top policy-making body), the ministry has twenty-one major units (not counting numerous affiliated trade corporations). Only three of the ministry's large subdivisions are regional/geographical departments. They deal with (1) the U.S.S.R. and other Communist countries in Eastern Europe and Asia; (2) Asia and Africa; and (3) North America, Latin America, Western Europe, and Oceania. The most important departments are those with functional responsibilities dealing with general imports and exports; technology imports and exports; international economic cooperation; international economic and trade organizations; laws and regulations; foreign trade administration (licensing); and foreign aid.

The other units deal with administration, support, training, and research. These include departments for policy research; planning; protocol; transportation; "the organization of production for export"; a general office; an education bureau; and an administrative department. The ministry also runs a university, a college, and three research institutes.

MOFERT, in sum, is an immense bureaucratic empire many times larger than the Foreign Ministry. Although it does operate within the framework established by overall policies determined by others (this is stressed by its leaders), and coordinates its policy at top levels with the Foreign Ministry and other institutions, the ministry now manages a very large area of China's foreign relations and plays a significant role in shaping policy in this area.

The Military Establishment

One of the most difficult questions to answer about the making of foreign policy in China is to what extent, and exactly how, the views of professional military leaders and experts influence foreign policy making.

Several things are clear. The military establishment is extremely powerful in China. Even though there has been a deliberate attempt since the early 1970s—and especially in recent years—to separate military and civilian affairs and to reduce the political roles of military leaders, the military establishment continues to exert a major influence on the making of policy—undoubtedly including foreign policy. It is also clear that many of China's top leaders tend to think about international problems in very broad geopolitical and strategic terms. And although, in making strategic judgments, they pay special attention to political and psychological factors affecting global trends and balances, they also give great weight to strictly military trends, factors, and balances. What is not very clear is exactly how the professional judgments of China's military specialists on these matters reach and influence either the top leadership or the civilian foreign affairs specialists who are primarily responsible for China's conduct of foreign relations.

What is striking when one examines China's apparatus for foreign policy making is how few professional military leaders or experts participate as regular members in the key civilian bodies responsible for making and coordinating foreign policy. As noted earlier, only one, Yu Qiuli, is on the Party Secretariat, and he is more of a political-military leader than a professional military man (no one to date has replaced Yang Yong, who was a professional commander), and the only one on the State Council is Defense Minister Zhang Aiping. None is in the core group of the Secretariat's Foreign Affairs Small Group, and none is on Ji Pengfei's foreign affairs coordinating group under the State Council.

It appears, therefore, that even though there are some links between the military establishment and foreign policy apparatus at lower working levels, these are relatively weak. The main channels through which the military establishment influences foreign policy appear to be at the very top of the system.

The Military Commission

Unquestionably, China's top military leaders have a very important and direct input into all policy-making, not only through Yu Qiuli at the Secretariat and Zhang Aiping at the State Council, but also directly from the highest military bodies to all the top civilian leaders and decision-making groups.

The Party Central Military Commission (Zhongyang Junshi Weiyuanhui, also translated as "Military Affairs Commission"), headed by Deng Xiaoping, is the highest authority in China's military establishment. The fact that Deng still heads it not only guarantees that its views are heard but also that the decisions of the top civilian Party leaders are communicated to and followed by the military establishment. (In 1982–83, the government established a parallel commission, but to date it appears to have maintained the same name, leadership, and personnel as the Party commission.)[52] The commission, and not the Ministry of National Defense, is the command center for the military establishment. Under it, the ministry is administratively in charge of matters such as the military budget and recruitment. However, though the defense minister is normally China's senior professional military leader, the ministry itself appears to be a less important institution in the actual running of the People's Liberation Army (which includes all major service arms) than three major departments that are said to report directly to the Military Commission: the General Staff Department (to which the commanders of the major service arms are responsible); the General Political Department; and the General Logistics Department. Relatively little is known, however, about the structure of these bodies and their interrelationships. Foreign experts differ, for example, on even such a basic question as whether the Military Commission has a large staff of its own, or relies for its staff work mainly on the ministry, or on the three general departments, or on all of these bodies.

Undoubtedly, the most important channel through which military views influence the foreign policy process in China is through Deng, although the members of the Military Commission, acting collectively or individually, also transmit their views directly to the top Party and government decision-making bodies (they sometimes sit in on meetings of these bodies as observers even when they are not members). In addition to Deng, the key men in this group are its four vice-chairmen—Ye Jianying, Xu Xiangqian, Nie Rongzhen, and Yang Shangkun—and its four deputy secretaries general—Zhang Aiping, Yang Dezhi, Yu Qiuli, and Hong Xuezhi. One striking thing about this group is the age of its members. Three of the vice-chairmen are old marshals (only one other surviving old marshal, Liu Bocheng, is missing from the group), and all are in their eighties—Ye is eighty-seven; Nie, eighty-five; and Xu, eighty-three. (As stated earlier, Ye is so ill that he is out of the picture, and it is probable that neither of the other two is very active.)

In reality, therefore, the key persons—apart from Deng—on the commission are Vice Chairman and Secretary-General Yang Shangkun (who, like the other vice-chairmen, is a Politburo member), and the four deputy secretaries general. Yang Shangkun—a man who has long been close to Deng—is labeled "permanent" vice-chairman as well as secretary-general. Although seventy-seven, he is still vigorous and obviously is the man who, working closely with the chairman, actually manages the commission's affairs. The four deputy secretaries general now include the heads of all the major hierarchies in China's military establishment: Defense Minister Zhang Aiping, Chief of the General Staff Yang Dezhi, and Yu Qiuli and Hong Xuezhi who head, respectively, the General Political Department and General Logistics Department. These men also are old—Zhang is seventy-four; Yang Dezhi, seventy; Yu, seventy; and Hong, seventy-one—and all probably will be replaced by younger men before very long, but there is no doubt that they will wield great power and influence as long as they occupy their present positions. It is reasonable to assume that when the views of these professional military leaders are communicated either through Deng Xiaoping or Yang Shangkun, or directly, they carry great weight in the policy deliberations of China's top civilian Party and government bodies on many issues. However, there is no way of knowing to what extent they involve themselves in—or are brought into—discussions of general foreign policy. Insofar as is known, the Chinese defense establishment has no office comparable to the Office of International Security Affairs in the U.S. Department of Defense, specifically responsible for relating military policy to foreign policy. Moreover, not very much is known about what kinds of research and analysis on military-strategic and political-military issues relevant to foreign policy are done by working-level professional analysts within the defense establishment to provide a basis for top military leaders—and top Party and government leaders as well—to make judgments on foreign policy issues that take military factors into account.

Political-military and Military-strategic Analysis

From what little is known, it appears that some research and analysis of this kind is carried out in several places. The G-2, or intelligence, organization (called the second division in China) of the General Staff Department is one. Probably most of its work focuses, however, on strictly military matters, including order-of-battle intelligence, rather than on analyses of broad political-military or military-strategic questions. The PLA's Academy of

Military Science is another center where considerable research and analysis takes place. However, according to informed Chinese, most if not all of its research focuses on military tactics and strategies rather than broad political-military matters. (This is even truer of the research carried on by the PLA's Military Academy and other training institutions.)

In 1979 the Ministry of National Defense established a new institute—the Beijing Institute for International Strategic Studies, which will be discussed later—with a mandate to carry on research on strategic questions and national security issues. However, although the institute is potentially important, it is still fairly small, and its research output is limited.

Elsewhere, in a few research institutes not directly linked to the military establishment, there are some academic specialists as well as government analysts (for example, in the Academy of Social Sciences' Institute of [North] American Studies, as well as the Foreign Ministry's Institute of International Studies) who deal with broad political-military and geopolitical issues. Some of the most interesting research of this kind may now be developing in these places, and, even though the quantity of such research is still limited, at least some of the studies resulting from this research reach political as well as military leaders and may influence their thinking on foreign policy issues.

All in all, however, it appears that (at least if one compares China with the United States and U.S.S.R.) only a limited amount of detailed research and analysis of broad political-military and military-strategic issues is done in China by working-level military professionals or civilian political-military analysts specifically to provide a basis for China's top decision makers (both political and military) to deal with foreign policy issues. One reason for this, some Chinese argue, is that, because China has not had global military involvements or commitments comparable to those of the superpowers, neither its political nor its military leaders have felt the same pressures as those affecting U.S. and Soviet leaders to encourage extensive, detailed political-military and military-strategic research and analysis. According to these Chinese, the civilians responsible for foreign policy in the Foreign Ministry and elsewhere have paid relatively little attention to military affairs, and military men in the defense establishment have paid relatively little attention to most foreign policy issues. Consequently, although the decisions made by China's top leaders are obviously based in part on their personal judgments on key military-strategic issues, many of these judgments may be made without much specific research and analysis—whether by military or civilian professionals—at lower levels, relevant to broad military-strategic problems.

Routine Political-military Coordination

In certain of its relationships—for example, with the United States—China faces an increasing number of foreign policy issues that, of necessity, are of direct concern to both the civilian foreign affairs specialists and the military establishment in Peking, and must involve both. The recent steps taken by China and the United States to expand military contacts, cautiously but significantly, provide a good example. Not only have military contacts been a subject of continuing discussion between Chinese and American political leaders and diplomats, but the development of Sino-American relations in the military field has increasingly involved direct military contacts—and military exchanges—between the two countries. Obviously, the basic decisions concerning military contacts and ties have been made at the highest levels in both countries, but, at an operating level, as exchanges have increased between the two countries' military institutions and personnel, new problems of coordination have developed. There is some evidence that in China (as in the United States) there are different views on how far (and how fast) military links should be developed—differences both within the defense establishment and between military leaders and civilian specialists on foreign affairs.[53]

These trends undoubtedly have stimulated efforts to strengthen liaison and coordination between the Foreign Ministry and Ministry of National Defense. Senior Foreign Ministry officials argue that liaison mechanisms are already adequate; not only, they say, are there links between top officials in the two ministries, but, when necessary, working-level Foreign Ministry personnel, even at the desk level, deal with counterparts in the National Defense Ministry either directly or through the Defense Ministry's Foreign Affairs Bureau (although the bureau concerns itself mainly with contacts with foreign attachés and military personnel visiting China). They point out, also, that when Chinese military leaders have made important trips abroad (as, for example, when Defense Minister Zhang visited the United States in 1984), a Foreign Ministry representative has gone along (although it should be noted that the Foreign Ministry representative was relatively junior and that liaison between the two ministries was said to be far from perfect).

However, the problems of routine coordination between the Foreign Ministry and China's military establishment will probably grow in the period ahead, and so far the links between the two ministries do not appear to be very close or effective. The involvement of the defense establishment in the foreign policy–making process still appears to be mainly at the top of the system, therefore, and it is not clear that even at that level there is any systematic effort—based on thorough research, analysis, and staff work at the lower levels—to combine the political-diplomatic and military-strategic perspectives of professionals at the two ministries in formulating foreign policy.

Political-military Coordination in Crisis Situations

Although the above discussion of China's routine political-military coordination appears valid in light of the available information, it leaves unanswered some important questions about how Chinese diplomatic and military initiatives have been coordinated during conflicts and crises. Since the Communist takeover in 1949, China has been involved in a number of major conflicts and crises on its periphery—in Korea and the Taiwan Strait area, on the borders of India and the Soviet Union, and in Vietnam. In most of these instances there appeared to be fairly close and, in many respects, effective coordination of diplomatic and military initiatives. At least in crisis situations, the nature of the coordination suggests that the Chinese leadership has been able to coordinate political and military moves in ways that cannot be fully explained by the available information on the existing institutional mechanisms in China for coordination. A key explanation, undoubtedly, is that in such situations political and military leaders at the highest levels of the regime engage in very close coordination, but exactly how this has been translated into close coordination at the lower levels of China's massive and complex bureaucracy remains unanswerable on the basis of what is now known.

Cultural Aspects of Foreign Policy

Any complete account of China's foreign affairs apparatus would have to include an analysis of the roles of the many government and nongovernment institutions involved in "cultural affairs." Since its inception, the Chinese Communist regime has regarded "people's diplomacy" as an important part of its foreign relations. In recent years, more conventional educational, scientific, technical, and cultural exchanges have become increasingly numerous and important. Although the institutions that implement these programs do not play primary roles in formulating foreign policy, they nevertheless play roles of some importance in the conduct of China's foreign relations, and there doubtless is some feedback from their activities that influences the policy-making process.

A complete list of organizations involved in this field would be very extensive and would have to include numerous Party organizations, journalistic and media agencies, "mass" organizations, professional societies, religious groups, academic institutions (including the Academy of Sciences and Academy of Social Sciences), and so on. Within the government, the most important institutions involved include the Ministry of Education, the Ministry of Culture, and the State Scientific and Technological Commission. (The activities of the above organizations encompass all the activities that in the U.S. government are conducted by the U.S. Information Agency, and much more.)

In general, it appears that coordination among these varied organizations is reasonably good. Although not all the coordinating mechanisms and procedures are known, one measure of their effectiveness is the consistency with which activities in all of these areas generally conform to current political policies.[54] It is known that

Foreign Ministry officials maintain close liaison with key people in the major ministries, commissions, and academies that manage exchange programs. There is also information on some Party as well as government agencies that supervise journalistic organizations. However, there may also be mechanisms—perhaps under the Party—that are not well known, to supervise and coordinate the foreign activities of other diverse organizations—for example, China's numerous "mass" organizations.

It is impossible to discuss here the many institutions and programs in this field that influence China's foreign policy in one way or another. However, a few comments will be made about two very close affiliates of the Foreign Ministry: The Chinese People's Institute of Foreign Affairs (Zhongguo Renmin Waijiao Xuehui, or CPIFA) and the Chinese People's Association for Friendship with Foreign Countries (Zhongguo Renmin Duiwai Youhao Xuehui, or Friendship Association). Both are headed by senior retired diplomats and are staffed in large part by personnel from the Foreign Ministry and other government foreign affairs organizations. (There is a constant interchange of personnel between the Foreign Ministry and these bodies. They are integral to the Chinese foreign affairs system, even though they are classified as "people's" or "mass" organizations.)

The CPIFA's origins date to the early days of the regime, and many of China's top diplomats have been on its board of directors. In recent years its principal function has been to develop high-level "nonofficial" exchanges with Western countries. A large percentage of the individuals it invites to China are prominent out-of-office statesmen, legislators, and politicians. A few are well-known foreign academics. The institute also participates in two-way exchanges and conferences with leading foreign affairs groups in Western countries. In the case of the United States, CPIFA has developed exchange programs with groups such as the National Committee on U.S.-China Relations, the United Nations Association/USA, the Aspen Institute, and similar groups. It also has hosted delegations from multinational organizations. The exchange programs of CPIFA do not involve large numbers of people, but Peking regards them as particularly important.

CPIFA's current president is Han Nianlong, seventy-four, one of China's leading diplomats since the 1940s. Han was a leading member of the "Executive Headquarters," established in 1946 during the Marshall mission to supervise the Guomindang-Communist truce agreed upon at that time. Subsequently, he was ambassador to Pakistan and Sweden in the 1950s. In the late 1950s and early 1960s he was an assistant to the foreign minister and rose to be a vice foreign minister just before the Cultural Revolution. Also, as stated earlier, during the talks to "normalize" U.S.-China relations in 1978, Han and Vice Foreign Minister Zhang Wenjin were Deng Xiaoping's principal aides in the final negotiations with Ambassador Leonard Woodcock. Today, Han, as an advisor to the Foreign Ministry, is still involved in many important foreign policy decisions.

Although the CPIFA is a relatively small organization, its hierarchy includes four vice-presidents (one of whom is a former ambassador to the United States, Chai Zemin), and its staff is divided into several operating divisions, the most important of which are organized by geographical regions.

The Chinese People's Association for Friendship with Foreign Countries is a larger organization, and in fact, it really is a "mass" organization for the conduct of "people's diplomacy." Established in 1954 as the Chinese People's Association for Cultural Relations with Foreign

Countries, it became the Chinese People's Association for Cultural Relations and Friendship with Foreign Countries in 1966, and then assumed its present name in 1971. Over time, it absorbed a variety of other organizations involved in the Communist-sponsored world peace movement and the movement for "Asian-African solidarity." It draws its personnel from the Ministry of Culture and other government bodies as well as from the Foreign Ministry.

Wang Bingnan, seventy-eight, who currently heads the association, joined Zhou Enlai's personal entourage when he participated, under Zhou's direction, in the Communist group that went to Xian in 1936 at the time of Chiang Kai-shek's kidnapping to try to promote a second united front against the Japanese. Subsequently, during the Sino-Japanese War, he was with Zhou in Chongqing, the Nationalists' wartime capital, where he was a secretary to Zhou and one of his press spokesmen. Thereafter, he was a key member of the small group of senior foreign affairs specialists closely associated with Zhou (others included Zhang Hanfu, Chen Jiakang, and Qiao Guanhua). Briefly, in the 1940s, he was a deputy director of a Central Committee Foreign Affairs Section. After 1949 he was chief, for five years, of a foreign affairs staff unit under Zhou, and accompanied Zhou as an advisor to the Geneva Conference and other major meetings. He rose at that time to be an assistant to the foreign minister. Subsequently, he was appointed ambassador to Poland and was the principal Chinese negotiator in the U.S.-China talks at Geneva and Warsaw. On returning to China, he was appointed as a vice foreign minister. Today, he is still actively involved in foreign policy decision making.

The Friendship Association is a large organization. Run by a group that includes 8 vice-presidents, a

number of secretaries-general, and a Standing Committee of 13, it has a staff of more than 300, divided into 7
divisions, 5 of which are regional (which closely parallel
those in the Foreign Ministry) and 2 of which are
functional (one for "publicity" and "cultural work," and
another that handles administration and logistics). According to Wang, the association now has ties with more
than 160 nongovernmental organizations in about 80
countries. Every year it invites roughly 300 foreign
delegations, including about 3,000 people, to China. It
also sends a few Chinese delegations—currently about ten
a year—abroad; normally each of these is headed by an
association vice-president. The association also organizes
exchanges of performing arts groups and exhibitions, and
is in charge of developing "sister" relationships between
Chinese cities and provinces and appropriate counterparts
in foreign countries (there are now more than 100 agreements for "sister" relationships of this sort). The Friendship Association participates in a few conferences with
public affairs organizations in Japan, Germany, the United
States, and some other countries (in the United States, the
Georgetown University Center for Strategic and International Studies [CSIS] is one of these), but this is a less
important part of its program than in the case of CPIFA.

Probably its most important and extensive exchange
programs are those involving bilateral cooperation between Chinese friendship associations established to deal
with particular countries or areas and their counterparts
abroad. From the early 1950s on, China established
many such associations. At the start, the Sino-Soviet
Friendship Association was by far the most important,
but over time many others were established to conduct
"people's diplomacy" throughout the world. These, like
so many institutions in China, virtually went out of

existence during the Cultural Revolution, but since the mid-1970s many have been revived and some new ones organized.

Wang's overall Friendship Association runs all of the subsidiary associations that handle bilateral relations with particular areas or countries. Each of the bilateral associations has a separate name and its own "leading body" and officers. However, according to Wang, "all of the day-to-day work of these associations is done by our association. . . . It is impossible to hire staffs for all of them, so we do the actual work of these associations."[55] (In the case of the United States, the Chinese umbrella association deals with the U.S.-China People's Friendship Association, but the Chinese are now considering whether or not to set up a subsidiary bilateral association in Peking to develop these ties.)

In sum, the Friendship Association and its affiliates handle a large portion of international bilateral activities that fall into the category of "people's diplomacy." Recently, a number of new institutions have been set up in this field—such as, the Chinese Association for International Understanding—but the Friendship Association will doubtless continue to be preeminent. While it will remain essentially a policy-implementing group, functioning as an adjunct to the Foreign Ministry, its leaders—so long as they are senior diplomats of Wang's caliber—will doubtless play a role in policy-making.

8.
OTHER SOURCES OF
INFORMATION
AND ANALYSIS

The Press

THE PRESS AND OTHER PUBLIC MEDIA influence the foreign policy process in every country. This is certainly true in the United States, where press reporting and editorials not only affect public opinion but also have a direct influence on both Congress and the executive branch; although leaders in the White House and State Department do not rely on the press for information on world affairs to the extent leaders do in China, they do read carefully the summaries of press opinion provided to them.

In China, the roles of press organizations and journalists in the policy process appear to be more direct and more influential. The special importance of NCNA's *Reference Materials* to leaders and policymakers has already been discussed. However, this is by no means the only channel through which the press and individual journalists affect thinking and decisions on foreign policy—not to mention the implementation of foreign policy. Leading journalists are active members of the foreign policy community in China. Top leaders of press organizations often sit in on meetings where decisions are made or articulated. Although they normally are invited to such meetings to ensure that they understand current policies (which they can then interpret authoritatively for both domestic and foreign audiences), their views may occasionally affect policy. Leading journalists maintain that, when policies are being formulated and thus are still being debated, journalists sometimes have considerable leeway in interpreting and articulating differing views on policy options and often can articulate their own views. There is some interchange of personnel between media organizations and the Party and government, and a considerable number of foreign affairs officials and academic specialists in foreign affairs were once journalists. There clearly is a very close relationship between media organizations and key policy-making bodies in the Party and government. Sometimes, heads of press bureaus serve as China's top representatives abroad in situations where China lacks official diplomatic representation.

In relation to foreign policy, the two most influential Chinese press organizations are the New China News Agency (Xinhua She or NCNA) and the *People's Daily (Renmin Ribao)*. Both play important roles, but their roles are somewhat different.

NCNA's origins date to 1931, when a "Red China News Agency" was founded in Ruijin (Jiangxi Province); it adopted its present name in 1937. It became a state agency in 1949. Ever since then, it has been the principal government organ for gathering and disseminating news at home and abroad. In the government hierarchy, its status is now the equivalent of a ministry. (Like all media organizations in China, NCNA is supervised by the Party Central Committee—in particular by the Propaganda Department's News Bureau and the Foreign

Propaganda Small Group—but NCNA staff members emphasize that it is part of the government structure rather than the Party apparatus.)

The top hierarchy in NCNA (as of mid-1984) consists of its director-general, Mu Qing; editor in chief, Feng Jian; general manager, Yang Jiaxing; and secretary-general, Guo Chaoren. According to NCNA staff members, its director-general and sometimes other leading editors and writers often sit in on important government meetings.

The staff of NCNA is very large, totaling more than 5,000 people at home and overseas. Abroad, the agency has more than 90 bureaus, with over 300 staff members. The relationship between NCNA's staff members—both correspondents abroad and its editors and reporters in Peking who deal with international news—and the foreign affairs apparatus in Peking is close. Not only, as stated earlier, have NCNA staff members sometimes served as Peking's top representatives in areas where China has no diplomatic ties (for many years this has been true in Hong Kong), but agency correspondents abroad often write authoritative commentaries on Chinese foreign policy.

At its Peking headquarters, three general offices are in charge of agency work: the General Editorial Office, the General Management Office, and the General Administration Office. Under these bodies, the organization has four major editorial departments that deal with domestic news, international news, domestic news for the overseas service, and "reference materials." There is also a department responsible for news photography and another that handles sports news, in addition to four support departments for technical matters, logistics, personnel, and the agency's own "foreign relations." In addition, it runs its own Journalism Research Institute, a staff training college, a publishing house, and a printing establishment.

The output of NCNA includes its daily *Xinhua News Bulletin,* aimed at foreign audiences, which is published in Chinese, English, French, Russian, Spanish, and Arabic and is distributed from centers in Hong Kong and fourteen foreign cities. It contains news and features on both domestic and international affairs.

Its other publications (totaling more than twenty, according to a 1984 report distributed by the organization that describes its activities), include *Economic Information* (*Jingji Cankao,* a daily, circulation about 500,000), *Outlook* (*Liaowang,* formerly a monthly but now a weekly on current affairs, circulation roughly 300,000), the *Globe* (*Huanqiu,* a monthly on international affairs, circulation about 500,000), *Fortnightly Review* (*Banyue Tan,* a biweekly mass publication on current affairs, circulation 3.5 million), and *Journalism* (*Xinwen Yewu,* a specialized monthly, for journalists).

Two of NCNA's subunits in Peking are key ones in relation to international affairs. One is the International News Editorial Department, which has two sections, one responsible for its world service in foreign languages, the other for dissemination of international news in China. The department has a staff of more than 400 in Peking and receives more than 100 stories daily from correspondents abroad. Its world service puts out a daily file of forty to sixty stories on international affairs. Its domestic service provides foreign news to all Chinese newspapers. The other department of special importance is the Reference News Department, which publishes not only *Reference Materials* (*Cankao Ziliao,* discussed earlier), but also a larger publication for Chinese subscribers called *Reference News* (*Cankao Xiaoxi*).

NCNA plays two important roles relevant to the foreign policy process in China. The first is to articulate and interpret Chinese policies for audiences at home and abroad, and the second is to gather and disseminate to China's elite information on world affairs, especially through the publications of the Reference News Department.

The extremely important role played by *Reference Materials* in informing China's top leaders and specialists in foreign affairs about developments abroad has already been discussed. The other major daily publication of this department, *Reference News,* is also very important, but in a different sense. Although *Reference News,* like *Reference Materials,* has been classified as an "internal" publication, its classification is much less restrictive (comparable to the low-level classifications of "official use only" or "limited official use" in the U.S. government). Moreover, Chinese newsmen state that it is to become an "open" publication in 1985. Like *Reference Materials, Reference News* carries articles from newspapers and journals abroad, but it is smaller and much more selective in its coverage. It is not distributed through organizational channels, as *Reference Materials* is; instead, people who wish to receive copies must subscribe to it. (Although some reports several years ago indicated that it was quite expensive, cadres state that a subscription now costs about 0.50 yuan a month, making it affordable for most Chinese who have any interest in it.) What is most remarkable about *Reference News* is its huge circulation, which is in the millions and for many years has been larger than that of *People's Daily,* China's most important national newspaper.[56] Most Party and government cadres in China, including local rural cadres at the grass-roots level, can subscribe to it, and a sizable percentage of them apparently do so. (It probably is accessible to a large percentage of China's 20 million Party and government cadres.) In urban areas, a large percentage of intellectuals reportedly see it regularly, as do many workers. Since *Reference News* carries much more foreign news than papers such as *People's Daily*, it is the main window on the world for most of the political, economic, and social elite in China. It is therefore one of the main sources of information shaping Chinese "public opinion" on world affairs. It is rather extraordinary that the "informed public" in China appears to get more of its news on world affairs from foreign articles carried by NCNA's *Reference News* than it does from Chinese newspapers.

The *People's Daily* plays a less important role than NCNA in informing China's elite about international affairs but an equally or more important role in articulating official policy within China. As an official organ of the Central Committee, it is the Party's principal national newspaper. It is one of the two main Party publications (the other being *Red Flag, Hongqi,* a Central Committee journal) that carries the most authoritative statements on Chinese policies.

The paper has a long history, and is the successor to a number of Party papers published under various names before 1949. Under its present name, it began publication in mid-1948, as the organ of the Central Committee's North China Bureau, which in mid-1949 moved to Peking, took over the Guomindang's paper there, and shortly thereafter became the Central Committee's official organ. The editors of the *People's Daily* emphasize its special status in the Party. They maintain that, although it is closely linked to the Central Committee's Propaganda Department, its position parallels that of the Propaganda Department.

The paper is printed in Peking and twenty-one other Chinese cities, and, according to staff members, currently has a circulation of roughly five million. Its staff now totals 1,900, more than 600 of whom are reporters and editors. Its leaders clearly belong to the top Party elite, and therefore they are to a certain extent involved in the formulation, as well as the implementation, of policy. Until 1983 the paper was headed by Hu Jiwei (who was reported to have been ousted or to have resigned because of policy differences with certain Party leaders). Now Qin Chuan is director (having replaced Hu Jiwei), and Li Zhuang is editor in chief; both have had long careers in propaganda work.

The paper's staff is divided into eleven departments which handle (according to a brochure put out by the paper in 1983) general editing, domestic politics, international affairs, mass work (dealing with readers' letters), education and science, rural work, industry and commerce, literature and art, general reporting, theoretical articles, and commentaries. Apart from the general editing department, those handling international affairs and commentaries are the key ones dealing with foreign policy–related issues.

The International Affairs Department, currently headed by Jiang Yuanchun, has a staff of about 130. It receives dispatches from more than thirty correspondents stationed in over twenty foreign capitals and Hong Kong. Two of the paper's eight pages (pp. 6 and 7) are devoted primarily to foreign news—and, in addition, of course, some important international news articles appear on the first page, and often these spill over onto page 4.

The international news carried by *People's Daily* comes not only from its own correspondents but also those of NCNA. Editorial staff members of the International Affairs Department state, also, that they read most if not all of *Reference Materials* every day before deciding which international news items the paper will carry. Such decisions are made, they say, in a series of daily editorial meetings. There is a "pre-editing meet-ing" of all the paper's principal editors every day at 5:00 P.M. Key people in the International Affairs Department also hold daily meetings. Decisions on late-breaking news are made by a department editor in charge for that day—often in the early morning hours—sometimes after telephone consultation with the department head.

Editorial staff members stress that, while the editors must be certain that the paper's articles reflect official policy, they can and do exercise some editorial discre-tion. This is particularly the case, they say, when policy guidelines are very broad, or when policies are still being discussed prior to the issuance of definitive positions by the top leadership. This, plus the participation of staff members in some high-level policy-making meetings, gives them some opportunity to voice their views in the policy process.

Clearly, however, the paper's main function is to articulate and interpret policies in an authoritative way once China's top leaders have defined them. Especially important in this respect are the paper's editorials, "commentator" articles, and "observer" articles. The most authoritative statements carried in the paper on policy issues or ideology are editorial department articles *(benbao bianjibu)*, but they appear only very rarely (the last one was in 1977). Regular editorials *(shelun)* written under the direction of the paper's editorial committee working in close consultation with top Party officials, are the most authoritative policy statements that appear frequently, according to staff members. Unsigned "com-mentator" articles *(pinglunyuan)* are almost equally au-thoritative (though they do not have the same kind of collective top-level endorsement that editorials do). Other commentaries and signed articles are less so, since they may reflect the author's individual views to a certain extent. Articles labeled "observer" *(guanchajia)* pieces are usually fairly long, analytical pieces, and they, too, are authoritative, but they have been rare in recent years. Editors of the paper state that, whereas formerly certain articles in some of these categories were written anonymously by top Party leaders, this is no longer the case, and that all such articles are now written by staff members of the paper (although, in the case of all important ones, they are written on the basis of close consultation with leading Party officials).

Even though the primary function of the *People's Daily* is to articulate official policy rather than to gather and disseminate information on international affairs, some of its leading editors and correspondents are important members of the foreign affairs community in China, and they participate in various ways in the foreign policy process.

Research Institutes

While the press is a major source of the "raw" information on world affairs that reaches China's policymakers, several institutes in China's research community produce a large percentage of the analytical studies of international problems and foreign policy issues on which top leaders as well as foreign policy specialists in the government rely. This research community is sizable and growing. Partly as a result of the expanding contacts between Chinese institutes and foreign affairs specialists in foreign countries, the sophistication of Chinese research specialists on foreign affairs in these institutes is increasing, and because of the new recognition on the part of Chinese policymakers of the importance of professional expertise, the contribution of members of China's research community to the policy-making process appears to be growing.

There are many research institutes in China that produce analyses that are fed into the foreign policy process. These include, for example, many that deal with economic problems relevant to foreign policy making, and one institute located outside of Peking (the Shanghai Institute of International Studies)[57] that deals broadly with international affairs. However, the most direct input into the foreign policy process is provided by several institutes in Peking. Three of these are "independent" institutes closely affiliated with the government: the Foreign Ministry's Institute of International Studies, the Institute of Contemporary International Relations, and the Beijing Institute for International Strategic Studies. The others are the institutes dealing with international affairs in the Chinese Academy of Social Sciences.

The government-affiliated institutes serve, first of all, as research arms of the government bodies with which they are linked, but their reports also go to other ministries and reach top Party and government leaders. They themselves initiate some of their studies, but they produce others in response to direct requests from Party or government leaders. Probably the majority of their staff members come from the government bodies with which they are affiliated. Almost all of their research is policy-oriented in a very specific sense. Most of it is classified, but two of them also publish journals aimed at the general foreign affairs community, and members of their staffs frequently write for other journals and newspapers.

The institutes of the Chinese Academy of Social Sciences (CASS) have substantially expanded their research in recent years. There are now eight CASS institutes whose principal responsibilities relate to foreign affairs (as well as some others who do research relevant in some respects to foreign policy issues). These include one that deals broadly with international economics and politics and seven that focus their research on particular regions or countries. Although part of their function is to carry out basic research on international problems and educate the public, they, too, produce a great deal of policy-oriented research, sometimes on their own initiative and sometimes in response to requests from Party and government leaders and foreign affairs specialists. Many of their reports (and journals), like those of government-affiliated institutes, are classified.

The Institute of International Studies (Guoji Wenti Yanjiusuo) is the principal one directly linked to the Foreign Ministry. It is the successor to an institute established under a different name (International Relations Research Institute) in 1956. Closed in 1967, during the Cultural Revolution, the institute was revived in 1973 under its present name and has been especially active since 1978. The staff of the institute totals about 250, of whom more than two-thirds are researchers, a majority of them former employees of the Foreign Ministry. There are senior and associate research fellows, assistant research fellows, and research fellows—with roughly equal numbers in each category. Most of the institute's staff members belong to divisions working on particular areas: the Americas (North and South); the Soviet Union and Eastern Europe; Western Europe; East Asia and the Pacific (including Japan and Southeast Asia); and West Asia, Africa, and the Middle East (a division which also covers South Asia). The institute also has a division that addresses international economic issues, and another ("comprehensive research") that deals with broad international issues—including security matters. The institute has a sizable library of its own, with more than 200,000 volumes, and it publishes its own journal, *International Studies Research (Guoji Wenti Yanjiu)*, established in 1960, halted in 1965, and revived in 1981. A few of its staff members hold concurrent faculty appointments at academic institutions, including Peking University and the Foreign Ministry's Foreign Affairs College.

The director of the Institute of International Studies is Zheng Weizhi, a senior retired diplomat. After serving in Chinese embassies in Indonesia and Pakistan, Zheng was ambassador to Denmark. He returned to Peking to head the Foreign Ministry's Department of American and Australasian Affairs in the 1960s (at which time he was in charge of the Peking end of the Sino-American talks in Warsaw while Wang Bingnan was handling the actual talks in Warsaw). The institute's deputy directors include Pei Monong, who deals with East Asian and broad international issues; Guo Fengmin, a specialist on Western Europe; and Hu Zhengqing, a specialist on the United States. The chief editor of the institute's journal is Xue Mouhong (who also is in charge of a major project to produce for the Foreign Ministry a history of China's foreign relations since 1949 based on archival materials as well as studies written by leading diplomats, both active and retired). Some of its staff members dealing with U.S. affairs have been stationed in the United States or have done research in American institutions.

The Institute of Contemporary International Relations (Xiandai Guoji Guanxi Yanjiusuo) is the largest research institute in China in the field of international affairs. According to its director, its origins are traceable to the 1940s, although since that time it has undergone several reorganizations and changes of name. A brochure published by the institute states that, in its present form, it was first established in 1964–65, was partially (but not totally) inactive during the Cultural Revolution, and assumed its present title in 1980.

At present, it is directly affiliated with the State Council and is responsible to the council's Center of International Studies, headed by Huan Xiang. (Some informed Chinese state, however, that it now also has links with the new Ministry of State Security, which was established in 1982–83.)

The staff of the Institute of Contemporary International Relations has a total of about 300 researchers and support staff members. According to its director, however, many of these are junior people, and the senior research fellows (the top rank for researchers) may not be much more numerous than their counterparts in the Institute of International Studies. The research staff is divided into eight divisions. One carries out "comprehensive research," with the remaining seven focusing on specific geographical areas: North America; Latin America; the Soviet Union and Eastern Europe; Western Europe; East Asia; South and Southeast Asia; and West Asia and Africa. Each division has a staff of about thirty. The institute publishes a journal entitled *Contemporary International Relations (Xiandai Guoji Guanxi)*.[58]

The director of the institute is Chen Zhongjing, who started his career with the Party during the Sino-Japanese War. After spending a short period of time at Columbia University in the 1940s, he returned to work in the Foreign Ministry in Peking. Thereafter, for most of his career, he was a deputy head of the Chinese People's Association for Cultural Relations with Foreign Countries (later the Chinese People's Association for Cultural Relations and Friendship with Foreign Countries), up until the Cultural Revolution. After the Cultural Revolution, he was engaged in research for the Central Committee for a period of time, and in 1980 was appointed to his present position. The institute has at least two deputy directors, Li Zhuang (in charge of day-to-day management) and Ren Pinsheng.

Until recently, the Institute of Contemporary International Relations had virtually no contact with foreigners and therefore was less well known than the other major research institutes in Peking. Now, however, it, like the others, is beginning to develop foreign exchanges and is more open than was previously the case. It clearly is a major source for foreign policy studies that go directly to China's top leaders. Because of its size as well as its direct links to the State Council and top Party and government leaders, its studies may in fact reach a broader range of leaders than those of some of the other institutions.

The third of the principal, government-affiliated institutes in Peking dealing with international affairs is the Beijing Institute for International Strategic Studies (Beijing Guoji Zhanlue Yanjiusuo, sometimes also referred to in Chinese as the Beijing Guoji Zhanlue Wenti Xuehui, or the Beijing International Strategic Studies Association). Established in 1979, it is the newest and smallest of the three, but clearly it is of importance because of its direct link to the Ministry of National Defense and the General Staff Department. Its constitution states that it is "an academic body for research on international strategic problems" established "to study strategic questions in relation to national security and world peace and to develop academic exchange with strategic research establishments, organizations, and academics abroad."[59] It is beginning to develop five projects relating to the strategic and security situation in Southeast Asia, Soviet military aims and activities in the Asian-Pacific region, trends and conflicts in the Middle East,

U.S.-Soviet strategic relations (including arms control), and the U.S.S.R.'s relations with Western Europe.

Currently, the institute's staff is quite small, totaling only thirty or so persons, of whom only twenty are working staff, including both administrators and researchers (the rest are institute "councillors"). However, some members of the institute clearly are in a good position to affect the thinking of Chinese military leaders. A majority of its staff, in fact, consists of officers, some retired but others still holding important positions in China's military establishment. Its director is Wu Xiuquan, a retired military leader who has held many posts relating to foreign affairs—particularly those concerning the U.S.S.R. and the international Communist movement—as well as high military posts. Immediately after 1949, he headed the Foreign Ministry's Soviet and East European Department, and in 1950 he was a member of both the Chinese delegation that accompanied Mao to Moscow (when the Sino-Soviet alliance was concluded) and the delegation that Peking sent to present its case to the United Nations. He was then appointed to be a vice-minister of foreign affairs, and in the mid-1950s he became China's first ambassador to Yugoslavia. Subsequently he was deputy director of the International Liaison Department, and continued to play a leading role in China's relations with Communist countries. Until recently, Wu was a deputy chief of staff in the General Staff Department as well as head of the institute. His senior deputy in the institute, Xu Xing, also has been a deputy chief of staff, and some of the institute's other staff members divide their time between the institute and the G-2 division of the General Staff Department. The secretary-general, who manages the day-to-day affairs of the institute, is Xu Yimin, who formerly served as defense attaché at the Chinese Mission to the United Nations and then at the Chinese embassy in Washington.

How much real research this institute, with its small staff, actually does, however, is unknown. It does not publish, and it appears, in fact, that perhaps its main function at present is to develop contacts with specialists on strategic and national security problems abroad; members of its staff have attended a number of international conferences. However, individual members of the institute clearly are in a position to influence China's top military leaders—and other leaders as well—on strategic issues that relate to foreign policy, and over time it may well develop into a significant research institution. (Although it has no plans at present to expand its own staff significantly, it plans to invite more "outside personnel" to participate in its work.)

One of the most important recent developments in the Chinese research community concerned with foreign policy issues has been the rapid expansion of research on international affairs carried out by the Chinese Academy of Social Sciences (Zhongguo Shehui Kexue Yuan), in large part as the result of the efforts of Huan Xiang, when he was vice-president of the academy, with the support of key staff members such as Zhao Fusan, a deputy secretary general of the academy (and its director-general for international exchanges).

The academy is a relatively new body. Although for many years there had been a Department of Philosophy and Social Sciences under the Chinese Academy of Sciences, it was only in 1977 that a separate academy for the social sciences was created, with Hu Qiaomu as its first president. (It is now headed by Ma Hong, a specialist on economic management.) The establishment of this academy gave a strong boost to the development in China of the social sciences in general and research on international affairs in particular. Starting with sixteen research institutes in 1977, the academy (according to a June 1984 academy report) now has thirty-two, plus three research centers and a postgraduate school. It has a total staff of more than 5,000, of whom about 3,000 are researchers and other professionals. Of the thirty-two institutes, eight now deal with international affairs, and today these are the principal academic centers in China for foreign policy–related research. These institutes are just beginning to publish part of their research output; a majority of their studies, reports, and journals are still classified. As is the case with the government research institutes, some of their studies are written on their own initiative, and others are produced in response to requests by Party or government officials dealing with foreign affairs. Key leaders and well-qualified specialists from these institutes as well as the government institutes are invited to participate in some important meetings of policymakers, such as those of the Party's Foreign Affairs Small Group, when issues on which they have special expertise are discussed.

One of the academy's eight international affairs institutes—the Institute of World Economy and Politics (Shijie Jingji Yu Zhengzhi Yanjiusuo)—deals with broad international problems that cut across regional boundaries. This institute was established in 1981 as a result of a merger of two separate organizations: the Institute of World Economy (set up in 1964) and the Institute of World Politics (founded in 1978). Its staff now totals roughly 230, of whom about 150 are research professionals. Much of its work focuses on economic issues, in divisions that deal with economic theory, comparative economic development, international economics, and major economic problems. It stresses research on world economic trends that it believes have important implications for world politics, including

North-South economic relations and problems relating to world food, energy, and technology transfers. There is less research, at present, on world politics per se; so far, there are fewer researchers in this area, and they have not been grouped into subdivisions. A primary focus of the institute's political research, according to its director, is on U.S.-Soviet relations and the relations of both superpowers with their allies.

Pu Shan is director of the Institute of World Economy and Politics. He obtained his Ph.D. in economics from Harvard in the 1940s and then returned to China to become one of the young men Zhou Enlai gathered around himself as assistants and secretaries. Like several others in this group, he participated, as a secretary to Zhou, in the Geneva and Bandung conferences. For a period, he was a member of the Foreign Ministry's Foreign Policy Research Office, and thereafter he spent many years on the staff of the ministry's Institute of International Studies, rising to become a deputy director before he replaced Qian Junrui as director of the Institute of World Economy and Politics.

The seven other CASS institutes dealing with international affairs are all area-studies institutes. They cover the Soviet Union and Eastern Europe; (North) America; Japan; Western Europe; West Asia and Africa; Latin America; and South Asia. Each has several research divisions, a small library, and a documentation center, as well as editorial and administrative offices. Reportedly, each produces a journal, but most of these are internal publications.

The strength of these institutes varies, but most of them appear to be expanding their staffs and broadening their research quite rapidly. The Institute of (North) American Studies (Meiguo Yanjiusuo), for example, started only a few years ago with a handful of members, and, although still relatively small, it is steadily developing staff members qualified to analyze American politics, U.S. foreign policy, the American economy, and American society and culture. It also has acquired the core of a staff (headed by Zhang Jingyi) to work on military-strategic issues, which already is the main center within the academy for work on such issues.

The director of the institute is Li Shenzhi. As mentioned earlier, Li belongs to a group of wartime graduates from Yanjing University who became associated with Zhou Enlai at that time. Li started as a journalist, working first for the *New China Daily* (others on its staff included Qiao Guanhua and Zhang Hanfu) and then NCNA, and in the 1950s was a secretary to Zhou Enlai and accompanied him to the Geneva and Bandung conferences and served as one of his speechwriters. After being victimized during the Anti-Rightist Campaign in the late 1950s, he resumed work for NCNA in the 1960s but was not fully utilized again until the late 1970s. He accompanied Deng Xiaoping to the United States in 1979 and then was chosen by Hu Qiaomu to organize and head a new institute to study the United States. Li is one of the Academy of Social Sciences specialists in international affairs who is invited on occasion to participate in meetings of policymakers, such as those convened by the Foreign Affairs Small Group; his views on foreign policy clearly carry weight in China's foreign affairs establishment.

Although it is difficult to judge precisely the extent to which these CASS research institutes influence China's policy-making process, their roles clearly are significant. More than is the case with the publications of most comparable institutions in the United States, some of the studies and reports of the CASS institutes feed directly into the policy process and reach top leaders. Moreover, institute directors and some of their most talented staff members appear to be respected by Party and government officials dealing with foreign affairs, and top policymakers often appear to take their views seriously into consideration.

Intelligence

Apart from the research-and-analysis institutions described above, it simply is not possible to identify with confidence what other organizations in China may be a part of the intelligence-gathering and analysis apparatus relevant to decision making in foreign affairs. The Chinese system clearly has always had some specialized bodies engaged in both intelligence and counterintelligence, but Chinese are unwilling to discuss them.

It is difficult to judge, therefore, exactly how large, or how important, these may be. On the basis of the public record, there appears to be nothing comparable to the large "intelligence community" that exists in the United States (which includes institutions such as the Central Intelligence Agency, National Security Agency, Defense Intelligence Agency, the army, navy, and air force intelligence organizations, the Federal Bureau of Investigation, and the State Department's Bureau of Intelligence and Research, as well as mechanisms that, at least in theory, coordinate foreign intelligence from all of these sources) or in the Soviet Union (where the KGB is a huge organization with primary responsibility for extensive intelligence-gathering as well as operations both abroad and at home).

Nevertheless, Chinese leaders undoubtedly do receive classified intelligence information and analysis on foreign affairs from agencies other than those already described, and it is reasonable to assume that these agencies are comparable at least in some respects to intelligence bodies in other major countries. Informed foreign analysts believe that, in the past, the Central Committee's Investigation Department and the Ministry of Public Security (plus the intelligence arms of the PLA) have been the primary intelligence agencies. These analysts also believe, however, that in 1982–83, when the new Ministry of State Security was established, it assumed primary responsibility for foreign intelligence as well as counterintelligence, taking over most, if not all, of these functions previously carried out by the Party's Investigation Department and Ministry of Public Security. The Ministry of State Security is reported to have a staff of foreign affairs specialists whose research and analysis is made available to China's top leaders and policymakers. However, on the basis of what little is known, it appears that China's foreign intelligence apparatus may be relatively small, at least in comparison with those of the two superpowers.

Universities

Although it is beyond the scope of this discussion to describe in detail the research and training conducted in China's major universities in the field of foreign affairs, a few comments on the role of these universities are required. In the long run, China's universities (especially its major "comprehensive" universities) are likely to play an increasingly important role in the Chinese foreign affairs community. To date, however, their roles appear to be less significant than those of institutions discussed earlier. Currently, the Party and government hire more specialists on foreign affairs from government training institutions than from major universities and rely more on research produced by specialized government research institutes and the Academy of Social Sciences than on university research.

Nevertheless, a number of China's universities are expanding their training and developing some systematic research relevant to foreign policy making. "International relations" is not a well-developed discipline in China, and there are significant programs labeled "international relations" in only two major institutions, Peking University and Fudan University (in Shanghai); in each case these programs are under a Department of International Politics. (Nankai University in Tianjin now is reported to be planning to establish a department or program in international relations.) However, a number of other universities have programs or courses that are very relevant to the study of international relations and foreign policy, and some of these are now developing specialized area-studies programs.

There are several kinds of courses relating to international affairs in Chinese universities. They deal with international relations theory (mainly Marxist-Leninist theory, based on the writings of Marx, Lenin, Stalin, and Mao; little attention is paid to Western international-relations theory), the history of international relations, world history, the foreign policies of China and other nations, the international Communist movement, political thought (including foreign political thought), international law, and world economics. The ideological component in such courses in Chinese universities is generally large, however—larger, Chinese foreign affairs specialists say, than in the activities of the research institutions discussed earlier. As contacts between Chinese and Western universities have grown, there have been some signs that scholars in Chinese universities are broadening their approaches to the study of international relations, but university professors still seem to be more inhibited in this respect than scholars in China's major research institutes.

Actually, the amount of research on international relations conducted at universities is still quite limited. The universities see their main function as one of training (especially to prepare students in this field for academic careers; relatively few seem to go into government careers). Here, too, however, there are signs of some changes, and a number of universities are beginning to develop research programs that could be significant, on foreign areas as well as on international law and economics and other relevant subjects.

In addition to Peking University and Fudan University, the other universities where considerable work on international relations, foreign policy, and area studies is developing include the People's University (in Peking), Nankai University (in Tianjin), Wuhan University, Heilongjiang University, Xiamen University, Jilin University, and Nanjing University.[60]

In addition to its international relations program, Peking University has programs dealing with international law and international economics and has established research centers that focus on international politics, international law, American studies, and South Asian studies. Fudan University, too, has special programs on international economics (it has a strong World Economics Research Institute and a research office dealing with the American economy). The People's University also specializes in world economics; its Department of Political Economy and its Foreign Economics and Management Institute are both large. It also has long had programs focused on the Soviet Union and Eastern Europe, and is reported to have established an Institute of Soviet and East European Studies. Nankai's special strength also is in economics (its Economics Research Institute has a very distinguished history); however, it also is strong in the fields of world history, including U.S. history. Wuhan's World History Department is considered by many to be the best in the country, and it also has one of the leading programs in China on American studies (reinforced by its Institute of American and Canadian Economic Studies and an Institute of American History). Heilongjiang has an Institute of Soviet Studies; Jilin, a Korean studies program; Xiamen, an Institute of Southeast Asian Studies; and Nanjing, a "research office" dealing with British and American foreign policy.

Even though these and other universities do provide much of the training available in China that is relevant to international affairs, and even though they do produce some research, university specialists still appear to be on the fringes of the foreign policy community in China—at least in comparison to specialists working in Peking's major research institutes. Nevertheless, the study of international affairs in China's universities is growing, and over time these institutions may acquire greater roles, more directly relevant to China's foreign policy community, primarily as training institutions but secondarily as centers for research.

The Foreign Policy Community

At several points in this study I have used the term foreign affairs or foreign policy "community." This requires some explanation, because one feature of the Chinese bureaucratic system that most impresses foreign observers is the degree to which Chinese organizations tend to function as "independent kingdoms."

It is true that, in the field of foreign affairs, as in other fields, the primary orientation and loyalty of most individuals is to their own "unit" *(danwei)*. As a consequence, institutional cooperation among units often is limited. Individuals tend to be identified with a particular unit for a very long period of time (in many cases, for their entire careers), and transfers of personnel are difficult to make. Moreover, the tendency of Chinese to think and operate in the context of vertical hierarchies *(xitong)* impedes lateral institutional contacts and cooperation between and among institutions.

Nevertheless, interviews with a wide range of Chinese involved in foreign affairs suggest that there is a group that can be legitimately regarded as a foreign policy community. The community is not large, and most of its members are based in Peking. However, it includes individuals who work on foreign affairs in many different institutional hierarchies. What makes it a community is that many, if not most, of its senior members know each other, are aware of the work and the views of other senior members of the community, and have fairly extensive contacts with each other—on a personal if not an institutional basis. The community includes a fairly wide range of leading specialists on foreign affairs who work for many Party and government institutions, research institutions of numerous kinds, journalistic organizations, and various nongovernment institutions that have contacts or activities abroad. They all rely fairly heavily on information provided by a limited number of public and "internal" publications that circulate widely within the community. A sizable number of the reports that they write also circulate fairly widely within the community. Many of the senior members of the community have personal ties that date back many years, and many of the most influential individuals among them have some institutional ties (for example, as fellow members of the boards of institutes such as the Chinese People's Institute of Foreign Affairs, the new Center of International Studies, and so on); the experts who are invited to participate in the meetings of bodies such as the Central Committee's Foreign Affairs Small Group are generally drawn from this group.

The community is by no means totally homogeneous or monolithic. Even though the range of permissible differences is much narrower than in pluralistic Western systems, individual members of the community do have different outlooks and disagree on policy issues, and there are inevitable rivalries among the institutions with which they are associated. Nevertheless, they interact constantly and influence each other, and collectively they help to shape "Chinese views" on foreign affairs and have a significant influence on the top Party and government leaders who make the major decisions on foreign policy.

9.
STRUCTURE, PROCESS, POLICY, AND POLITICS

T HIS STUDY, AS STATED EARLIER, examines only the structure and process of foreign policy making in China, not Chinese foreign policy per se or the politics of foreign policy making. It would be not only unjustifiable but foolish to try to deal with the latter subjects in any broad fashion as a postscript to the study. However, it is worth asking whether or not any of the major trends described in the study—for example, the shift in the locus of decision making at the top of the system, and the increasing regularization and professionalization affecting the policy-making process—have any relationship to, or implications for, the substance of policy and politics of foreign policy making in China.

Although it would be incorrect to maintain that changes in the way foreign policy is made necessarily affect actual policy, a good case can be made that the recent changes in the structure and process affecting the making of foreign policy in China not only have paralleled important changes in the substance of China's foreign policy but have been linked to them. They also

137

may have significant implications for politics affecting foreign policy making.

There have been some notable changes (as well as some important continuities) in Chinese foreign policy during the past few years, which the changes in the structure of foreign policy making have both reflected and reinforced. All of these have been rooted in the fundamental shift of emphasis that has occurred—from ideologically-motivated revolutionary policies to pragmatic problem-solving approaches and from revolutionary political goals to developmental economic aims—in China's overall approach to major problems both at home and abroad.

The adoption of a new foreign policy posture, labeled an "independent foreign policy," has been one of the most important of the changes. While national security continues to be the highest-priority foreign policy objective of Peking's leaders, China's approach to solving its security problems is now different in important respects from what it was in the past. Mao's basic inclination was to identify the "main threat" to China at any particular time and to pursue a "united front" strategy and confrontational tactics to obtain support from other nations to deal with that threat. In the 1950s China decided to align closely with the Soviet Union. When the Sino-Soviet split occurred, China adopted a confrontational posture toward both the superpowers during much of the 1960s. Then, in the late 1960s, when Mao decided that the Soviet Union posed the greatest threat to China, he returned to a united-front approach and leaned toward the United States in the hope that Washington would counterbalance the Soviet threat. This continued throughout the 1970s, even under Mao's successors and, in fact, reached a peak when Deng visited the United States, and Peking tilted strongly toward Washington in the late 1970s.

Since 1981–82, however, China has deliberately positioned itself between the two superpowers (a development that seems to represent a change of view on Deng's part). China still has much more important relations with the United States than with the Soviet Union, but Chinese leaders now have made it clear that they do not intend to align closely with either superpower and will try to avoid confrontational relations with both.[61] While continuing to expand their ties with the United States, the Chinese have gradually sought to reduce tensions and "normalize" relations with the Soviet Union, and in many respects they have disengaged from the U.S.-Soviet military-strategic contest.[62]

This posture is one that Chinese leaders believe serves their interests well, under existing circumstances. They still view the U.S.S.R. as the main long-term threat to China, and they still count on U.S. power to counterbalance and check the Soviets, but, by stressing their unwillingness to align fully with, or be subordinate to, any other power, the Chinese have adopted a posture that gives them greater maneuverability and flexibility in pursuing China's own interests, as they see them, on particular problems and issues.

An equally important recent development in Chinese policy has been Peking's adoption of an "open door" policy as well as the decision by Chinese leaders to place far greater emphasis on foreign economic relations, in order to support China's modernization. In economic terms, the significance of China's relations with Japan and Western Europe, as well as with the United States, has steadily grown. In addition, however, China has very pragmatically attempted to establish "normal" diplomatic and trade relations with virtually all nations, with little regard for the kind of ideological and political criteria that formerly had a much more significant impact on Chinese foreign policy; Peking now is expanding both its economic and political ties worldwide.

Chinese leaders now stress, also, that a "peaceful international environment" is necessary for China's own development, and their actions suggest that they really believe this.[63] China has become much more involved in the international community during the past few years than ever in the past. It has, for example, become a much more active member of the United Nations; it has developed extensive ties with the World Bank, International Monetary Fund, and many other U.N.-affiliated organizations; and it is beginning to play a more active role in international discussions of arms control issues.

Nationalism (or patriotism) has always been a powerful and basic force shaping Chinese foreign policy, but, if possible, it has become even more so as the influence of old ideological concepts has declined. Chinese leaders are especially sensitive to any issue that they believe involves "sovereignty"—which is one of the "five principles of peaceful coexistence" first articulated publicly in 1954 (and from the Chinese point of view, probably the most important of these principles). In 1984, on the thirtieth anniversary of the "five principles," Peking strongly reemphasized the importance of these principles in determining Chinese policy.[64]

Chinese nationalism and Peking's great stress on sovereignty clearly create some problems between China and certain of its neighbors which have conflicting views on issues that they, too, believe involve their sovereignty. However, even in regard to issues of sovereignty, Peking recently has shown increasing pragmatism and flexibility. The concept of "one country, two systems"—on which the Chinese now base their approach to both

Hong Kong and Taiwan, and which may have even broader application—is the most striking example of this. Under this formula, China has been willing to agree to very special arrangements for Hong Kong, for a period of at least several decades, so long as the principle of Chinese sovereignty is not challenged.[65]

Recently, the Chinese also put renewed emphasis for a period of time on their "theory of three worlds." First put forward by Mao in 1974, this theory emphasizes the long-term importance of the Third World.[66] It fell into the background in the late 1970s, but then began to receive renewed attention in the early 1980s when China began moving toward the adoption of an "independent foreign policy." At present, the theory no longer is emphasized (Chinese specialists on foreign affairs say its validity has been the subject of active debate); nevertheless, the Chinese again are emphasizing the importance of their relations with Third World countries, even though, in objective terms, China's relations not only with the superpowers (the "First World") but with the other developed nations (the "Second World") are of greater and more immediate importance to Chinese security and economic interests.

However, while China is again emphasizing its ties with the Third World, it now stresses intergovernmental relations and has virtually ended its encouragement of and support for revolutionary activities by Communist parties or other radical movements in Third World countries. To date, it has not been willing to end all ties with Communist parties that are in opposition to established governments abroad (and this continues to create problems in China's relations with certain Southeast Asian nations). Nevertheless, the stress in its current policy is almost entirely on the need to develop good relations with established governments (even those in countries where there still are Communist insurrections aimed at their overthrow).[67]

Together, the changes that have occurred in Chinese foreign policy make it significantly different from the past. There has been some opposition to certain changes—most of all to the "open door" policy, but probably also, on the part of at least a few, to the general trend toward pragmatism, the great stress on economic interests, the compromising approach embodied in the concept of "one country, two systems," the downgrading of ideological considerations, and the virtual abandonment of support for revolutionary movements abroad. However, the opposition has not been strong enough to block the new trends.

Clearly, Hu Yaobang and Zhao Ziyang as well as Deng have been strong promoters of the recent policy changes and are closely associated with them. The shifts in the roles of, and relationships among, China's top policy-making bodies have helped to overcome opposition to the changes, and the strengthening both of the personal roles of Hu and Zhao and of the institutions they head enhances the prospects for continuation of present policies after Deng passes from the scene. Perhaps, in the future, when most of China's Party elders are gone, there could be another shift in the relationships among China's top bodies, in which the Politburo and Standing Committee again would become the main bodies where most day-to-day policy decisions are made. If and when this does occur, however, the membership of these bodies doubtless will have changed, and, if Hu and Zhao are able to consolidate their positions when the post-Deng succession occurs, the future membership of the Politburo is likely to be weighted heavily in favor of individuals who support the continuation of current policies.

There is no question that China's new pragmatism helps to explain the increasing regularization of the foreign policy process and the recent trend toward professionalism and better utilization of experts of all kinds in China's foreign affairs community. There also is little doubt that most of China's foreign affairs professionals support most of the recent changes in foreign policy.

It does appear—as some Chinese in the foreign affairs community argue—that as recent trends have developed, the consensus supporting China's foreign policy has steadily broadened. Even though some opposition to certain policies continues, it is mainly latent. Whether there will be continuity of policy or major shifts in the years immediately ahead will doubtless depend, above all, on whether or not China's pragmatic reformers continue to dominate the leadership in Peking. It will also depend, however, on whether or not their policies are perceived to be successful. No one can predict with confidence either the ability of Deng's successors to lead or the likelihood that their policies will succeed. One can say, however, that on balance, recent developments enhance the prospects for continuity and success.

NOTES

1. The Party Secretariat was formally reestablished in early 1980 (although steps in this direction were taken somewhat earlier, and the formal decision to reestablish it was made at the Fifth Plenum of the Eleventh Central Committee). At that time, Politburo member Ye Jianying called the Secretariat a "first line" organization and said the Politburo was in the "second line." See Feng Jian and Zeng Jianhui, "Springtime in Zhongnanhai," *Liaowang (Outlook)*, 20 April 1981, in Foreign Broadcast Information Service (FBIS), *Daily Report: People's Republic of China*, 17 April 1981, K2. The role of the Secretariat increased thereafter. However, as late as 1982 the Chinese press continued to stress the primacy of the Politburo and Standing Committee. For example, an article in the Party's journal *Hongqi (Red Flag)*, no. 5, 1982 (translated in FBIS, *Daily Report: People's Republic of China*, 22 March 1982, K6) stated: "With the exception of some questions in daily work which the Central Secretariat is authorized by the Central Politburo to decide on and handle, the decisions made by the Central Secretariat on questions concerning major principles and policies must be approved by the Politburo and Standing Committee of the Politburo prior to circulation as central instructions." As late as the fall of 1982 Politburo member Hu Qiaomu still described the Standing Committee of the Politburo as "the leading core for the day-to-day work of the Party"; see Hu Qiaomu, "Some Questions Concerning Revision of the Party Constitution," in *Beijing Review*, no. 39, 27 September 1982, 17. These statements suggest that the shift of decision making from the Politburo and Standing Committee to the Party Secretariat and State Council, as described by Premier Zhao in the statements quoted below, probably has occurred since the Twelfth Party Congress in September 1982.

2. These and subsequent quotations from Premier Zhao Ziyang are from a personal interview I conducted with him in Zhongnanhai (headquarters for top Party and government leaders), Peking, on 19 July 1984. The interview focused on China's foreign policy. The text of that part of the interview dealing with the formulation of foreign policy was published in the *China Business Review* (September–October 1984), 56–57.

3. A comparable statement is attributed to Hu Yaobang, who is quoted as saying, "Even foreigners know that Comrade Xiaoping is currently the Chinese Party's chief policymaker"; see "Hu Yaobang Says: Comrade Xiaoping Is Currently the Party's Chief Policymaker," *Beijing Wenzhai Bao*, no. 95, 29 July 1983, 1, in FBIS, *Daily Report: People's Republic of China*, 8 August 1983, K1.

4. The judgments made throughout this study rely heavily on interviews and conversations with a wide range of Chinese officials and scholars, both in China and in the United States, during 1983–84—and especially on interviews held in Peking during July–August 1984. In general, however, I do not cite individual Chinese sources, except in a few instances when I quote them directly or feel it particularly appropriate to cite particular individuals. To indicate the range of people I interviewed, they included not only the premier but numerous individuals from the level of vice-minister to country desk head in both the Ministry of Foreign Affairs and the Ministry of Foreign Economic Relations and Trade, leaders and staff members of all the major government and academic research institutes discussed in this study, leaders in the Academy of Social Sciences and the directors and staff members of several of its institutes, a number of senior retired diplomats including those who now head the major cultural exchange organizations that are discussed in this study, and several top editors and correspondents in the *People's Daily*, New China News Agency, and All-China Association of Journalists. Earlier, I had interviewed a number of

leading Chinese university professors, as well as senior Chinese diplomats abroad. These interviews with Chinese who are part of China's foreign affairs community have provided the foundations for this study. In addition, however, I have drawn upon data and insights obtained from Chinese (in Peking and elsewhere) who have been longtime friends and acquaintances, from foreign diplomats in Peking, from U.S. government specialists in Washington, D.C., and from American academic and nonacademic colleagues and friends who have both studied and dealt with China in recent years.

5. A senior academic in one of the major research institutes in Peking stated the following to me, in July 1984: "The idea of 'one country, two systems' is an important concept. . . . Of course, for us the main purpose of this idea is to solve the questions of Hong Kong and Taiwan. . . . [But recently Deng said] it also relates to international, not just domestic, problems, to the question of how to solve international disputes in a peaceful way. He did not specifically mention Korea, but I personally think he meant Korea and Germany—and not only them. Deng said we must have new viewpoints to cope with new situations."

In the fall of 1984, Deng himself said to a group of foreigners and Chinese from Hong Kong and Macao, "We must always decide whether we are going to solve an international issue in a peaceful or nonpeaceful way. We must find a way to break deadlocks. When we worked on the idea [of 'one country, two systems'] we also took into consideration what methods should be used to resolve international disputes. So many issues all over the globe are tied up in knots which are very difficult to undo. It is possible, I think, that some of them might be untied through this method"; see *Beijing Review*, no. 44, 29 October 1984, 17.

6. For further discussion of the "open door" policy, see pp. 15–16 and 20ff.

7. The first official, public articulation of the concept of an "independent foreign policy" was in Hu Yaobang's "Report to the Twelfth Party Congress" on 7 September 1982. In this report, Hu said: "Being patriots, we will not tolerate any encroachment on China's national dignity or interests. Being internationalists, we are deeply aware that China's national interests cannot be fully realized in separation from the overall interests of mankind. Our adherence to an independent foreign policy accords with the discharging of our lofty international duty to safeguard world peace and promote human progress. In the thirty-three years since the founding of our People's Republic, we have shown the world by deeds that China never attaches itself to any big power or group of powers, and never yields to pressure from any big power." (See FBIS, *Daily Report: People's Republic of China*, 8 September 1982, K18.) According to knowledgeable Chinese, Hu Yaobang himself played a key role in defining this concept, but in addition, a significant role in the drafting of this particular section of the report was played by Politburo member Hu Qiaomu and specialists on foreign affairs from the State Council and Chinese Academy of Social Sciences.

8. Although Deng Xiaoping achieved primacy in the leadership at the Third Plenum of the Eleventh Central Committee in December 1978, it was not until the Fifth Plenum in February 1980 that the remaining individuals regarded as persons closely linked to Chinese "leftists" were removed from the Politburo (the little Gang of Four—Wang Dongxing, Wu De, Chen Xilian, and Ji Dengkui) and that Hu Yaobang and Zhao Ziyang (protegés of Deng who were soon to become Party general-secretary and premier) were promoted to the Politburo Standing Committee. Finally, at the Sixth Plenum in June 1981, Hua Guofeng resigned as Party chairman and was replaced by Hu Yaobang. In the late 1970s and at the start of the 1980s, Deng seemed able to dominate most policy-making in the fields of foreign policy and science and technology, but was less able to have his way in policy-making on economic issues and cadre policy. However, over time his policy views have increasingly prevailed in these fields too.

9. See, for example, Li Xiannian's interviews in late 1981 and early 1982, in FBIS, *Daily Report: People's Republic of China,* 20 October 1981, C1; 28 December 1981, C1; 8 January 1982, C1; and 13 January 1982, G1.

10. Major policy decisions also emerge from the plenary meetings (plenums) of the Central Committee (scheduled, according to the 1982 Party Constitution, to meet "at least once a year") and Party congresses (scheduled to meet at least "once every five years"). Generally, however, the policies that emerge from such meetings have been defined by the top leadership before the meetings are held. The importance of ad hoc Party work conferences, which played a greater role in policy-making in some past periods, especially in the 1960s, appears to have declined, but it is clear that various other kinds of ad hoc advisory meetings, and specialists meetings, are still important. (See, for example, the *Liaowang* article cited below in note 11.)

11. The text of this article, from which all the following quotations are drawn, is in: FBIS, *Daily Report: People's Republic of China,* 18 June 1984, K1–7.

12. The communiqué of the Third Plenum of the Eleventh Central Committee called for "actively expanding economic cooperation on terms of equality and mutual benefit with other countries on the basis of self-reliance, striving to adopt the world's advanced techniques and equipment and greatly strengthening scientific and educational work to meet the needs of modernization"; see *Beijing Review,* no. 52, 29 December 1978, 11. The foreign policy implications of this statement did not become fully clear, however, until later.

13. Some Western analysts believe that Xi and Yang (both of whom are very high-ranking Party leaders) were deliberately sent to be Guangdong officials by Deng to prepare the groundwork for the establishment of special economic zones.

14. "On the afternoon of the conclusion of the forum, Comrade Deng Xiaoping and Li Xiannian came specially to Huairen Hall to meet the comrades and take photographs with them in the garden of Huairen Hall"; see FBIS, *Daily Report: People's Republic of China,* 18 June 1984, K5.

15. The new Central Advisory Commission, according to the 1982 Party Constitution, "acts as a political assistant and consultant to the Central Committee" (members must have "a Party standing of 40 years or more"); see text of the Constitution, FBIS, *Daily Report: People's Republic of China,* 9 September 1982, K11. The aim of Deng and others in establishing the commission obviously was to provide a body to which Party elders could be honorably retired. See "Deng Xiaoping Speaks on the Nature of Central Advisory Commission and Matters that Merit Attention" in FBIS, *Daily Report: People's Republic of China,* 27 October 1982, K5–6.

16. As far as I am aware, the first occasion on which Hu and Zhao both chaired a top Party meeting was in late 1982. According to Chinese sources, the First Plenum of the Central Committee immediately after the Twelfth Party Congress "was presided over by Comrades Hu Yaobang and Zhao Ziyang"; see *Beijing Review,* no. 38, 20 September 1982, 5. This practice obviously is designed to underline the aim of creating a collective type of leadership, in which Hu and Zhao share power under Deng's aegis.

17. In my interview with Premier Zhao Ziyang on 19 July 1984, Zhao not only stressed that the "open door" policy is "not a temporary expedient"— rather, it is a long-term policy—but he indicated that China's aim is to expand steadily the opening to the West. "We are determined to press ahead," he said, "We will go further. . . . At first, we thought joint ventures should sell [only] to foreign markets. . . . We have discovered that the Chinese market is of most interest to foreigners, and we have decided that we will make available some Chinese markets to foreigners. . . . In the future what will happen is that the opening will spread to the interior; that is the tendency." (From my notes of the interview.)

18. Although official Chinese birth dates are now available for most Politburo members, for a few they are still lacking, and the dates for these vary (even among

different agencies in the U.S. government), so that the figure of seventy-four conceivably might be wrong by one year (or at most two years). The ages for individual leaders used throughout this study are the ages they reached at some point during 1984 (the available data give only the year of birth, not the month or day).

The biographical data on leaders and other Chinese (diplomats, academics, and so on) given in this study are from three sources: official Chinese biographies, biographical dictionaries published outside of China, and information obtained in my interviews with Chinese in Peking in July 1984. Brief but useful official Chinese biographies of most of the Chinese leaders I discuss can be found in FBIS, *Daily Report: People's Republic of China,* 13 September 1982, K4–7; 20 June 1983, K7–11; and 21 June 1983, K10–23.

Additional data, and information on Chinese not covered in the above sources, can be found in Donald W. Klein and Anne B. Clark, *Biographic Dictionary of Chinese Communism, 1921–1965,* 2 vols. (Harvard University Press, 1971); Union Research Institute, *Who's Who in Communist China,* 2 vols. (Hong Kong: Union Research Institute, 1969); and *China Official Annual Report, 1981* (Hong Kong: Kingsway International Publications, Ltd., 1981). Biographical data that I use which are not from these sources were obtained in interviews in Peking.

19. To some Westerners, a drop in average age from mid-seventies to mid-sixties may not seem like a "generational" change, but in the Chinese context it clearly is. All those who have been members of the top leadership group in China for most of the period since 1949 are now in their seventies or eighties; most took part in the "Long March." With the notable exception of Hu Yaobang, leaders who are now in their mid-sixties joined the revolution after the Long March.

20. See the text of the 1982 State Constitution in FBIS, *Daily Report: People's Republic of China,* 7 December 1982, K1–28.

21. Li Xiannian, seventy-five, first became a vice-premier in 1954, and thereafter his major government posts included the following: minister of finance, director of the State Council's fifth office (finance, trade, and food), deputy head of a group in charge of financial and economic affairs under the Central Committee, and vice-minister of the State Planning Commission. However, in the early 1960s, Li reportedly assumed responsibility for foreign affairs when the foreign minister was absent.

22. Just prior to 1949 Peng Zhen headed the Central Committee's Organization Department. After 1949 Peng was Party first secretary and mayor of Peking (from the early 1950s until the Cultural Revolution). He also was secretary-general of the NPC Standing Committee (which Liu Shaoqi chaired) in the 1950s. Elected to the Politburo in 1956, he became the second ranking secretary of the Secretariat (under Deng Xiaoping), and the only one besides Deng who was on the Politburo. He made a number of trips abroad in the 1950s and 1960s, and was involved in many talks with foreign leaders (especially Communist leaders). He played a major role in the Sino-Soviet debates at the start of the 1960s.

23. His brief Party history was published in 1951, on the eve of the Party's thirtieth anniversary, and was entitled *Thirty Years of the Communist Party of China.*

24. Unattributable interview, March 1984, with a Chinese who is himself involved in the foreign policy process in Peking.

25. Hu Qiaomu's influence may have been adversely affected to some degree in 1984 because of the role he played, together with Deng Liqun (head of the Central Committee's Propaganda Department), in the short-lived campaign against "spiritual pollution." It is debatable, however, how much Hu and Deng suffered politically at that time; both continue to have high Party standing and visibility (as of early 1985).

26. It is not clear how frequently or regularly Zhao participates in Secretariat meetings. It is difficult to believe he can find time to do so regularly. Nevertheless, it

is a significant fact that he can and does attend some Secretariat meetings—presumably when either he or Hu Yaobang considers it important for him to do so.

27. Feng Jian and Zeng Jianhui, "The Central Committee's Secretariat and Its Work," in *Beijing Review*, no. 19, 11 May 1981, 21.

28. The biographical data on Party Secretariat members that follow can all be found in the sources cited in note 18.

29. For an explanation of this change, which was instituted with the adoption of the Party's 1982 Constitution, see an interview with Hu Qiaomu, entitled "Some Questions Concerning Revision of the Party Constitution," in *Beijing Review*, no. 39, 27 September 1982, 15–29. Hu points out that the general-secretary now is responsible for "convening" the Politburo and its Standing Committee, and that "obviously, convening and presiding are different roles." The change, Hu Qiaomu said, "will help prevent the recurrence of overconcentration of personal power and arbitrariness of a single person."

30. See his full statement in the text of the interview; see note 2.

31. Zhao Ziyang in his interview with me stated, specifically: "Sometimes scholars also participate [in the Foreign Affairs Small Group], including scholars from the Chinese Academy of Social Sciences." (When saying this he nodded his head to two such persons who were present at the interview, Huan Xiang and Li Shenzhi, whose backgrounds and positions will be discussed later.)

32. FBIS, *Daily Report: People's Republic of China*, 4 May 1979, L13–19. I am indebted to Lyman Miller for calling the reference to this group to my attention. The so-called "three reconciliations," according to accusations leveled against Liu Shaoqi during the Cultural Revolution, were reconciliation with "reactionaries," "revisionists," and "imperialists," and the "reduction" referred to aid to revolutionary struggles abroad. Some Chinese specialists on foreign affairs state that what was discussed, but not adopted, at that time was a policy of three "peaceful" principles—peaceful coexistence, peaceful transition, and peaceful competition.

33. Donald W. Klein and Anne B. Clark, *Biographic Dictionary of Chinese Communism, 1921–1965*, vol. 2, 1092.

34. "Foreign Contacts of the Communist Party," in *Beijing Review*, no. 42, 15 October 1984, 19.

35. See Zhao interview cited in note 2.

36. For a listing of the full membership of the State Council appointed in 1983, see FBIS, *Daily Report: People's Republic of China*, 21 June 1983, K2–4. According to the 1982 State Constitution (Article 88), what I label the "inner cabinet" it calls the "executive meetings of the State Council," which it specifies should include the premier, all vice-premiers and state councillors, and the secretary-general; FBIS, *Daily Report: People's Republic of China*, 7 December 1982, K19. Currently the secretary-general is one of the four vice-premiers, Tian Jiyun.

37. This and the following quotations also are from the interview cited in note 2.

38. The biographical data that follows on the members of the State Council's "inner cabinet" come from the biographical sources cited earlier in note 18.

39. In September 1984, in what appeared to be a routine cabinet reshuffle, Lu Dong, sixty-nine, replaced Zhang as minister of the State Economic Commission. Lu's background is very similar to Zhang's. After holding many positions dealing with heavy industry, Lu rose to be a vice-minister in Zhang's commission, and now he has replaced him.

40. At the same time that Lu Dong replaced Zhang Jingfu, Fang Yi was replaced by Song Jian, fifty-two, an engineer whose previous post had been that of a vice-minister in the Ministry of the Aerospace Industry.

41. Donald W. Klein and Anne B. Clark, *Biographic Dictionary of Chinese Communism, 1921–1965*, vol. 2, 1102.

42. *Ibid.*, 1103.

43. *Ibid.*; see also A. Doak Barnett, *Cadres, Bureaucracy, and Political Power in Communist China* (New York: Columbia University Press, 1967), 3–9 and 456–59.

44. Interview with Vice-minister Jia Shi, Peking, 2 August 1984.

45. In October 1984 Gong Dafei was relieved of his post as vice-minister and appointed as advisor, so that then the ministry had two advisors. (Until recently, He Ying and Fu Hao also were advisors.)

46. In October 1984 all three assistant ministers (Zhou, Liu, and Zhu) were promoted to be vice-ministers. Undoubtedly, there will be new appointments to the rank of assistant minister.

47. In late 1984 Han Xu was reported to be slated to replace Zhang Wenjin as Chinese ambassador to the United States in early 1985.

48. Since becoming vice-minister, Zhu Qizhen reportedly has taken over the responsibilities that had been Han Xu's. Zhu has been succeeded in his former post as head of the Department of American and Oceanian Affairs by Zhang Wenpu, who had been his deputy and previously headed the U.S. desk.

49. The changes taking place in the college illustrate the general trend toward professionalism. In earlier years the college drew many of its students from military units and local governments. Now its students are younger and come with better educational qualifications. Students chosen for its five-year program are selected from middle-school students by a national competitive examination. Students for its two- to three-year graduate program are also carefully selected by examination from applicants who have B.A. degrees. The college is also broadening its programs. It now has about forty students taking M.A.s and Ph.D.s (mainly the former), according to its director, Liu Chen (interview in Washington, D.C., 25 October 1984). It also plans to invite senior diplomats (ambassadors and minister-counselors) to spend six months to a year at the college. It is developing some research activities. Currently, it has two research institutes—the Institute of International Law and the Institute of the History of International Relations (and houses the offices of the two national associations in these fields). The director says he hopes to send ten to twenty young faculty members and advanced students to the United States annually for training.

50. For background on this group, see Donald W. Klein, "The Management of Foreign Affairs in China," in John M. H. Lindbeck, ed., *China: Management of a Revolutionary Society* (Seattle: University of Washington Press, 1971), 305–11.

51. These and the following quotes are from my 2 August 1984 interview with Vice-minister Jia Shi in Peking.

52. In the interview cited in note 29, Hu Qiaomu indicated that for the present the membership of both military commissions may be identical but suggested, albeit somewhat ambiguously, that eventually there will again be only one Military Commission and that it will then be in the state apparatus rather than the Party apparatus. It is still not clear exactly what objectives lay behind the creation of the new government Military Commission. It appears to have been related to Deng's desire to redefine Party and government relations and to shift some functions from the Party to the government, but it is unclear whether or not an eventual shift of the Commission from the Party to the government was envisaged. No such shift has in fact occurred to date.

53. Officials in the Foreign Ministry appear to be more cautious about how far and how fast China should go in developing military links with the United States than are some leaders and officers in the PLA (although there also appear to be some differences within the PLA on this). These differences of opinion are strikingly

parallel to those in the United States, where many members of the State Department are cautious, while some (though not all) in the Pentagon wish to move rapidly ahead.

54. As was mentioned earlier, some Chinese state that there is a "small group" under the Central Committee that coordinates activities in this field. In the early 1980s, also, there were reports of a special unit in the government, headed by the then minister of culture, Huang Zhen, responsible for "external cultural liaison."

55. Interview with Wang Bingnan, Peking, 2 August 1984.

56. There are different figures on the circulation of *Reference News*. A deputy editor in chief of the *People's Daily* told me (in an interview in Peking, 23 July 1984) that it is now roughly 7 million, which he said is larger than the circulation of the *People's Daily*, which he put at about 5 million (a drop, he said, from about 6 million not long ago). A Western article published in 1984 cites a figure of 8.47 million for 1981, based on Chinese sources; see Jörg-Meinhard Rudolph, "China's Media: Fitting News to Print," *Problems of Communism* (July–August 1984), 64. However, a mimeographed report given to me by NCNA editors at their office gave the circulation of *Reference News* as 4.8 million which is the most up-to-date figure available.

57. The Shanghai Institute of International Studies is "under the guidance" of the Foreign Ministry, its senior staff meets periodically with persons from the Ministry and the Peking Institute of International Studies, and copies of the Shanghai Institute's books and reports go to them, but, because of distance, it largely operates on its own. (It is financed by the Shanghai government.) The institute, headed by an economist, Chen Qimao, has a staff of between fifty and sixty researchers, divided into five geographical sections: the United States, Soviet Union and Eastern Europe, Western Europe, Japan, and the Middle East. (Recently, the section dealing with the Middle East has expanded its staff and work to cover South Asia and Southeast Asia; a change in its name is under consideration.) The institute publishes quite extensively; among its publications is an annual yearbook on international affairs.

58. As was noted earlier, the institute also runs a training institution, the College of International Relations (see p. 90).

59. Constitution of the Beijing Institute for International Strategic Studies (in English, Beijing, no date), 5.

60. Douglas P. Murray, "International Relations Research and Training in the People's Republic of China" (Northeast Asia–United States Forum on International Policy, Stanford University, February, 1982), and Michael L. Baron, "The State of American Government and Law Studies in the People's Republic of China," (Research Report, Office of Research, United States Information Agency, Washington, D.C., December 1982) contain valuable data on international studies in Chinese universities and research institutions.

61. The Chinese began moving toward an "independent foreign policy" during 1981–82, a period when U.S.-China relations were severely strained because of the issue of U.S. arms sales to Taiwan. The problems in U.S.-China relations clearly were a factor, but not the only factor, impelling Peking to move in this direction. The shift seemed to reflect a broad reassessment of the global "balance of forces" and of China's interests. Some U.S. analysts argue that it also reflects a compromise and political balance at the level of the Standing Committee of the Politburo between the views of Deng Xiaoping, Hu Yaobang, and Zhao Ziyang on the one hand, and varying views of Li Xiannian and Chen Yun (and perhaps also Peng Zhen) on the other.

62. Both the Russians and the Chinese now seem committed to try to reduce tensions in their relationship, but neither expects any far-reaching rapprochement. The Chinese have put forward three conditions for any major improvement in relations—a reduction of Soviet forces around China, the end of Soviet support for

Vietnam and its occupation of Kampuchea, and a Soviet withdrawal from Afghanistan—which they doubtless recognize Moscow is unlikely to meet. Nevertheless, the recent improvements in relations (mainly in regard to rhetoric, trade, and exchanges) are significant and have changed the tone of Sino-Soviet relations. The Chinese also appear to have downgraded somewhat the immediacy of the Soviet military threat to China. However, they continue to see their U.S. tie as important to Chinese security (and are cautiously developing military contacts with the United States). There is, in sum, no prospect of any real tilt toward the Soviet Union.

63. China's continuing tough position toward Vietnam, and support for forces in Kampuchea which oppose the Vietnamese occupation, represent the one case where the Chinese now maintain a militant position. Long and complex historical factors help to explain this exception that proves the rule.

64. One Chinese article, commemorating the thirtieth anniversary of the "five principles," stated that Zhou Enlai first proposed the principles to the Indians during talks on 31 December 1953, four months before they were incorporated into a Sino-Indian agreement in late April 1954; Ling Dequan, "A Mighty Weapon for Safeguarding Peace—Adviser to the Foreign Ministry Ho Ying on the Five Principles for Peaceful Coexistence," in *Liaowang*, no. 17, 23 April 1984, in FBIS, *Daily Report: People's Republic of China*, 1 June 1984, A1–5.

65. For the details of these arrangements, see *A Draft Agreement between the Government of the United Kingdom of Great Britain and Northern Ireland and the Government of the People's Republic of China on the Future of Hong Kong* (London: Miscellaneous No. 20, 1984, Her Majesty's Stationery Office, September 1984).

66. Mao Zedong first articulated this concept of three worlds in a talk with a Third World leader in February 1974. The concept was first put forward publicly by Deng Xiaoping in a speech before the U.N. General Assembly in April 1974. In the immediate post-Mao era, a major article on the concept by the Editorial Department of the *People's Daily* gave it great publicity; King C. Chen, *China and the Three Worlds* (White Plains, N.Y.: M.E. Sharpe, 1979) 85–123. Soon thereafter, however, it was played down; it was then revived in 1981, but recently has received decreasing attention.

67. China has, for all practical purposes, ended active support of Communist insurrections in Asia. It still gives moral and political support, however, to the Arabs in their struggles with Israel and to Africans in their struggles against white regimes in southern Africa.

INDEX